Blind Chickens and Social Animals

Creating Spaces for Afghan Women's Narratives Under the Taliban

Anna M. Pont

Published by:
Mercy Corps
3015 SW First Avenue
Portland, OR 97201, USA
(800) 292-3355, ext. 250

ISBN 1-931573-00-X

Cover Design: Moondance Graphics
Cover Photo: Kim Johnston/Mercy Corps
Production Coordination: Alissa D. Zwanger

Printed in the United States of America

First Mercy Corps Printing: August 2001

November 2001

Table of Contents

Acknowledgements

I thank all the women who made this work possible by contributing their time, sharing their ideas, opening their homes and offering many cups of tea. In this regard I am particularly indebted to Dr. Yasmin Hamidi.

I would like to acknowledge the support and assistance of Mercy Corps' field and office staff and the Bureau of Population, Refugees and Migration of the US Department of State, which provided funding for Mercy Corps' assistance projects in southern Afghanistan.

A special thank you to the Country Director, Mark Pont, for his patience and encouragement.

Prologue

It is Monday. Women sit inside fanning each other with their loose large sleeves talking and laughing. Morning chores are finished. Older women greet me by kissing the top of my forehead, young girls kiss my hand. The hands of the mistress of the house are patched with blue black dye. She has been busy dyeing wool for weaving kilims. Another woman stretches out her hand too. There is a loose metal watch hanging around her wrist like a bracelet. It has a bright green face. "Look I need this now. I have places to be in, on time!" We sit down on mattresses on the floor, lean against the wall. I have brought a guest to see these women, who have formed, since 1996, the health committee in their village to discuss health issues with their communities. Half a dozen women, in brightly coloured dress, break the silence all at once.

"Tell her to ask us how we have changed. We have become more aware of everything – of ourselves. Even men don't beat us, as they sometimes did before. This is our time now. Before, we were like blind chickens, tell her; yes, like blind chickens. We didn't know anything. Now I give awareness to girls and other women about taking good care of themselves, even of their teeth, otherwise they will end up like me; toothless. That's what I tell them."

✻   ✻   ✻

A group of ten women are making two lists; what men do in one day and what women do in one day. We joke about how much longer the women's list is compared to the men's. As we begin to make a move, Mahgul suddenly raises her voice above the others and says, "Add this to the men's list: The men go out to the fields. When they come back, they sleep with us and enjoy us. They also have to make us happy!" There is hysterical laughter in agreement. It spills out into the paths outside the compound as women hurry home to cook lunch for men returning from their fields. Passing each other on the way home, women stop to greet each other. Invitations for visits to homes for a more relaxed gossip are extended. By the time we reach the home compound, the social calendar for the week seems full. I ask the two *chadars* billowing in front of me if they socialise with everyone in the village. Niekbakhta's comment sums it all up, "[I talk] to every woman and some men who are relatives, because we are social animals."

— 1 —

Introduction

The position of Afghan women has been widely discussed since the emergence of the Taliban in Afghanistan. In the current discourses on gender and women's position in Afghanistan, a voice needs to be given to local female interpretations of gender, female and male roles, needs, capacities, perceptions, and impacts of rights violations.

This study attempts to open discursive spaces for the narratives of Afghan women and to show the complexity and heterogeneous nature of women's position in Afghanistan today. It is the outcome of qualitative research commenced in March 1998 among Afghan women, both in southern Afghanistan and in refugee villages in Baluchistan, Pakistan.

Research was carried out among the predominantly Pushtoon population in rural areas of southern Afghanistan, which is the heartland of the Taliban. Rural women who live in Taliban-controlled areas were interviewed. Issues of female mobility, access to education and health care, women's activities and sources of information, female roles in economic and agricultural development, and repatriation were addressed. This focus reveals that the position of Afghan women is not uniform, nor are women passive bystanders.

Any research that investigates women's position cannot be divorced from issues relating to both men and women and the different roles that are played out in a community. This study is concerned with gender, however it does not claim to unravel the meanings of gender or gender roles in Afghanistan. Men were not formally interviewed in the course of the research.

Gender, in the context of this work, is defined as the cultural and social interpretation and understanding of biological difference. It is a social and symbolic arena of ongoing contestation over specific identities, behaviors, rights, obligations, roles, responsibilities, and sexualities (Butler 1990, Sedgwick 1990: 27-28). "Gender roles" are culturally specific differences between male and female gender. "Male" and "female" can be valued differently in different contexts and cultures. One gender can be accorded more power than the other in particular contexts. Male and female gender roles are elastic and interlinked with one another.

Speaking of gender in Afghanistan is entering into a very complex web of cultural practices, relationships of power, ethnicities, different religious interpretations, issues of nationalism, class, and economic status. Gender relations are not unified. Discourses of gender and power have been historically constructed, for instance by war.[1] The knowledge of sexual difference is: socially and politically constructed, present in institutions such as *purdah*,[2] and particular to the cultural structures of a given area.

Western discourse has a tendency to define the third world woman as a powerless victim of particular cultural, religious and socio-economic systems or of the colonial process.[3] It homogenises women. Historical and cultural analysis are invaluable in illuminating the complex and diverse nature of women's position in Afghanistan today, which leads to a fuller understanding of the impact of the Taliban on women.

Many restrictions on female mobility, visibility and work precede the emergence of the Taliban. Previous government authorities, not only the Taliban, have imposed some form of dress code on women and limits on women's movement. This is not a new phenomenon. Like many rulers before them, the Taliban link women's seclusion and the segregation of the sexes to nationalism, national development and cultural change.

II

For more than a century, the veil has been a potent signifier of the social meaning of gender, which influences political and cultural issues. The great social transformation and new ideological developments that resulted from European colonialism in the nineteenth and early twentieth centuries set the economic and political parameters for change worldwide. Even though Afghanistan was never colonised, the discourse that emerged during colonialism has had an impact on Afghanistan.

During western colonialism, Muslim women in the Middle East and South Asia became a central subject of national debate as issues concerning women became linked with nationalism, national development and cultural change. The discourse that emerged stated that to improve women's status in the colonies, the "innate" and "irreparable" misogynist practices of the native culture needed to be abandoned for European customs and beliefs. For the Muslim world, this implied replacing Islamic-style male dominance with western-style male dominance (Ahmed 1992: 127-129). Or creating, as Nair (1992: 30) puts it, "western style order out of eastern style chaos."

In this discourse, Islam became linked to the oppression of women. The use of the veil and the segregation of the sexes were seen as the fundamental reasons for the backwardness of Islamic societies. It was implied that the only way a Muslim society could develop and become "civilised" was for these practices to be abolished. Thus, the veil was a symbol of the oppression of women and the backwardness of Islam (Ahmed 1992: 162-164).

Subsequently and conversely, as this colonial narrative on women and Islam entered the mainstream Arabic discourse, the veil became a symbol of resistance to western domination and liberal society, best known in the cases of Algeria, the revolution in Iran, and now most recently in Afghanistan. In this resistance narrative, the veil symbolises the dignity and validity of all "native" practices, particularly those that have come under attack during a previous regime or an outside influence (Ahmed 1992: 162-164. See also Arendt 1985, Afkami 1995, Bhahba 1994, Nair 1992, and Said 1991). As we can see in Afghanistan today, many of these practices are those relating to women's position, mobility and dress. The impact of Taliban-imposed restrictions have been most severely felt in urban centres where populations were accustomed to freedom of dress, movement and employment. Many of these urban women have expressed their views and objections to Taliban edicts. Rural women who live in Taliban-controlled areas have had less of an opportunity to be heard.

---

[1] The 1970s saw growing political tensions in Afghanistan. This resulted in the coup d'e-tat of April 1978 and was followed by the Russian invasion in 1979. The war with Russia continued until the withdrawal of Russian troops in 1989. The Soviet-backed government of Najibullah followed and lasted until 1992. After the collapse of this government, civil war commenced as rival Mujahedin groups vied for power. This continued until the Taliban takeover of Kabul in 1996. The civil war between the Taliban and the Northern Alliance continues to present.

[2] Female seclusion and segregation of the sexes.

[3] See Mohanty 1994, Jayawardena 1995, hooks 1981, 1994.

— 2 —

The Taliban

The Taliban began as a small spontaneous group in Kandahar in 1994. Their leader, Mullah Mohammed Omar, had been a commander in the Mujahedin Hisb-e-Islami (Khalis) party. In 1994, the Taliban took over Kandahar, a city that had been in a state of anarchy for two years due to different Mujahedin groups fighting for control. The Taliban disarmed the population and announced their plan to bring peace and create a true Islamic state based on Shari'ah law in Afghanistan. By February 1995, the Taliban had taken over almost half of the country, but it wasn't until September 1996, when they took Kabul, that the Taliban hit world consciousness (Marsden 1999: 43-58).

The Taliban prescribed codes of behaviour and dress for men and women. A higher degree of religious observance was required. Men were instructed to pray in the mosques rather than at home. All non-religious music was banned, as was any visual representation of the human or animal form. These edicts were based on a very conservative interpretation of Islam.

The Taliban considered cities, Kabul in particular, as centres of liberalism, decadence, and the origins of political parties and factions that had caused the downfall of Afghanistan. Therefore, the edicts of the Taliban had to be implemented rigorously in the urban areas while the more conservative rural areas, where the Taliban had their power base, were largely left to themselves. Maintaining strict observance of the edicts of dress and behaviour in urban areas became important for the Taliban, as these are areas where opposition is likely to arise (Marsden 1999: 57-66). These edicts focused the world's attention on Afghanistan as women in Kabul and other cities experienced serious rights abuses.

In southern Afghanistan, Pushtoons, who are the predominant ethnic group, enjoy security if they behave according to the edicts of the regime. The situation is presently somewhat different for ethnic minorities. Though the Taliban insist that the movement is open to all ethnic groups in Afghanistan, its interpretation of Islam is Sunni. Therefore, in practice the movement does not embrace the Shia populations of central Afghanistan, namely Hazaras, or the Ismailis of the northeast (Marsden 1999: 44).

Despite where their sympathies and support may lie, no women are members of the Taliban movement. Afghans, particularly women, distinguish between who *is* Taliban, and who *is taken* by Taliban. Fighting along with the Taliban does not mean that one is Taliban. The Pushto expression *Taliban saradi* means "with Taliba" and is used to refer to those men who have joined the political movement. *Taliban ackhestidi* means "taken by Taliban" and is used to refer to those men who are fighting within the Taliban forces but who are not Taliban. For instance, some men, such as Shah Bibi's husband who has no land of his own, work with the government though he himself is not Taliban. "My husband is working with the government and the business of poppy . . . taking poppy to Pakistan," Shah Bibi (45, HAZ 54).[4]

The priority of the Taliban is to bring the whole country under its control. There is no apparent agenda to spread beyond the existing borders of what is known as Afghanistan. The aim is to purify Afghanistan. As the governor of Kandahar metaphorically explained in 1998, "When we took over, the 'house' was a mess. It was necessary to take strict measures to bring our house into order. Once the house is in order, one can then start to develop things and relax."

In this aim to conquer and purify Afghanistan, all other matters such as employment, education and functioning services remain low priorities. These issues are on hold until the successful conquest of the entire country (See Dupree et al. 1999, Marsden 1999).

---

[4] 45=Age, HAZ 54=Location and Code Number. See Appendix III.

— 3 —

Research Methodology

The Pushtoon

The majority of the women in this research are Pushtoon. As an ethnic group, the Pushtoon[5] are spread across the southeastern parts of Afghanistan, the northwest frontier province of Pakistan, and the tribal areas along the border between the two countries. The 25 million Pushtoon are made up of approximately 50 different tribes, the most famous of which are the Durranis, Afridis, Khattaks, and Waziris. The Pushtoon on both sides of the border have three fundamental elements in common: religion, the Pushto language, and the Pushtoon cultural system of morality, modesty and the law of honor, known as the *pushtoonwali* or *pukhtu*.

Islam constitutes a spiritual and worldly way of life. The Pushtoon, regardless of nationality, consider each other brothers in faith to whom hospitality and help is owed. The war against the communist government and the Soviet invasion was considered to be a holy war, *jihad*. Despite some local variations and dialects, the Pushto language is spoken by all Pushtoon. The family household is the primary social, economic and political frame of Pushtoon life, as well as the unit of production and management. Households are patrilineal and patrilocal[6] and are also considered the fundamental unit of solidarity and cooperation.

Pushtoonwali is based on such core values as honour and modesty. Hospitality and blood revenge are other crucial aspects of "having" or "doing" *pukhtu*. Hospitality and refuge must be granted to anyone who seeks it. People compete for the reputation of being hospitable. *Badal*, blood revenge, is central to understanding most action and interaction within Pushtoon society; it is an honourable act to kill someone who has killed one's relative. This complex system of morality and law of honour define the individual and the space they are accorded in society. Women are closely guarded and secluded as carriers of family and male honour (Ahmed 1976, Boesen 1983, 1988, and Grima 1993: 2-6).

A woman's virtue is linked with maintaining the Muslim social order in tact. Seclusion is a way of protecting both men and women from each other and their innate natures and instincts.[7] It reaffirms the social order of the family and the hierarchy of the social world outside the home. As wives, daughters, and sisters, women hold the dangerous position of being able to disrupt bonds between men, the harmony of the household, and ultimately of the whole community. In some cases *purdah* has become a way of keeping women dependent on male relatives and has been used to deny women access to economic, social and political power (Mernissi 1987).

There is a reciprocal relation between *purdah*, the seclusion of women and the segregation of the sexes, and *izzat*, male and family honour and respect. The institution of *purdah* demarcates boundaries in the context of gender and mobility. These boundaries can be divided into boundaries of physical space and boundaries created by dress and behavior. Restrictions on women's freedom are important because the Pushtoon form a society where men expect to find a virgin bride. Women's seclusion is strictest during adolescence. Family honour is maintained and enhanced through a daughter's marriage. A married woman is guarded and protected by her husband and *affines*,[8] particularly her mother-in-law. After giving birth to children, restrictions on her movements begin to relax. A woman is least tied down by *purdah* restrictions after menopause, her "loss of sexuality."[9]

The *Pushtoonwali* is not a homogeneous and consistent cultural system. It contains inherent dilemmas and contradictions, interpretations and choices, which must be understood in specific contexts.[10]

The war, and now the Taliban, have molded and influenced the cultural and social structures of Afghan Pushtoons.

Research Locations

The research was carried out in Helmand province of Afghanistan and the refugee villages in Baluchistan, Pakistan. In Afghanistan, interviews were carried out in the capital of Helmand province, Lashkargah City, and four districts within Helmand: Garamser, Nad-i-Ali, Nar-e-Saraj and Nawsad. The pre-war estimated population of Helmand province was 397,000 people, 94 per cent of whom were considered rural (Scott 1980). The refugee villages in Baluchistan include: Pishin, Killa Abdullah, Zhob, Chagai, and Loralai districts (for maps see Appendix II).

Since early 2000, all of these research areas have suffered, to a lesser or greater degree from the onset of drought. There has been inadequate rain over the past year to replenish the aquifers, rivers and dams that feed into the irrigation schemes on which these populations and their crops rely.

Bust District

The estimated population of Bust district, where Lashkargah is situated is 67,962 (USAID census 1990 plus growth rate 1.92). Tribally, it is predominantly Barakzai, Achekzai, Popolzai, and Isakzai.

Before the war, Lashkargah City was called "little America" due to the large North American community who were there to develop infrastructure: irrigation canals and drains. In the 1950s and 60s, the Americans built the town: residential areas, hospitals, cinema and other "modern" services. Later it was inhabited by an increasing number of Afghans from all over the country and suffered destruction during the years of fighting. One Kandahari pilot remembers Lashkargah as everyone's favourite place to be posted. "Lashkargah was little America, now it is like a graveyard," Eqlima (38, Las 8).

Garamser District

Garamser district is situated along the Helmand River. The Darweshan and Shamalan canals run through the area. The estimated population of the district is 54,037 (USAID census 1990 plus growth rate 1.92). The areas in Garamser where research was carried out include Hazarjuft, Darweshan, Shamalan, Kharai, Deh Zekria, Laki, and Loy.

The population of Garamser is very heterogeneous. In the 1950s, landless families from the north, east and central areas of the country were brought there and each given 30 *jeribs*[11] of land to cultivate. Due to this, the population of Garamser is made up of many different ethnic groups and Pushtoon tribes. The indigenous Pushtoon tribes of the area are Barakzai, Alikozai, Nurzai, Achekzai, and Popalzai.[12] Different ethnic groups in the area include Hazara, Tajik, Turkoman, and Uzbek. Nomads that travel through Garamser are Pushtoon and Baluch of the same tribes as the settled populations.

Agriculture is the main source of livelihood in the area. Due to the dryness of the area, many families are also engaged in livestock production. The Hazarjuft bridge and hospital were rehabilitated by Mercy Corps.[13] The bridge re-opened the southern trade and access route between Iran and Pakistan. The interviewees in Hazarjuft acknowledged this,

"The hospital and bridge – without question, everybody is benefiting, especially women and children," Bibi Borjana (30, DA 4).

"Every single person has benefited from the bridge," Bibi Nahida (20, LO 3).

Nar-e-Saraj District

Grishk is the largest town in which research was carried out. It is located in the Nar-e-Saraj district, which has an estimated population of 86,919 (USAID census 1990 plus growth rate 1.92). The central town is on the Kandahar-Herat road along the Boghra canal. Villages spread across both sides of the canal. Due to the 75km Boghra canal and the closeness of the Helmand river, Grishk has agricultural land that was allocated to landless people from other areas of Afghanistan by the government. The population of Grishk is made up of Tajiks, Uzbeks, Hazaras, and many Pushtoon tribes: Alizai, Nurzai, Achekzai, Muhammadzai, Popalzai, Barakzai, Alkozai, Kharut, Daftani, and Sulemankhel. Though not a majority, the Muhammadzai, the King's tribe, have the most influence and power in the area, as they own the most land.

Nad-i-Ali District

Nad-i-Ali, a district along the Lashkargah Grishk road that is about 40km from Lashkargah City. It has an estimated population of 62,645 (USAID census 1990 plus growth rate 1.92). The Boghra and Darweshan canals run through the district and enabled agriculture to become the main source of livelihood. The early settlers to the area were Pushtoon nomads but migration to the area increased as the area prospered due to improved farming. The population of this district is ethnically diverse due to the Government resettlement of many landless families from the north. There are people of the Kharoti, Arab, Kakar, Achekzai, Nurzai and Baluch tribes (Scott 1980: 7-8).[14] The central town has a small bazaar of approximately 150 shops. Small villages spread out on both sides of the road.

Nawsad District

Nawsad is a predominantly Pushtoon area north of Grishk. It is conservative and was not as much affected by the war as the areas of southern Helmand. Therefore, the population, which is predominantly Isakzai, Barakzai and Alikozai, has remained fairly stable with very little migration or repatriation from surrounding countries. During the war, the population of the area traveled from one village to another avoiding the worst of fighting. Very few left the area as refugees. The area's current estimated population is 50,222 (USAID census 1990 plus growth rate 1.92).

Villages in Nawsad are placed in valleys around stony flood washes. Individual compounds, orchards, and even some of the fields are hidden behind high mud walls. Tight serpentine roads work their way around people's dwellings and agricultural land. There is an adequate supply of water by *karez*[15] but these are often destroyed by spring floodwaters and affected by ground water levels.

Pishin and Killa Abdullah Districts

There are three refugee villages in the Pishin and Killa Abdullah districts of Baluchistan. They are Saranan, Surkhab and Pir Alizai. All three villages started off as refugee camps but with time, the Afghans have built mud houses and the camps have become permanent settlements that are now called refugee villages. The total population of these three camps is 93,246 people. Of these, 18,710 are adult women and 27,668 are girls under the age of fifteen (Mercy Corps Census 1999).

Saranan and Pir Alizai are both situated in very dry desert areas. The Saranan camp is divided into two: old and new Saranan. Surkhab is larger than the other two camps and spreads out 13 km across a dry riverbed in a valley. Only in Surkhab do a few green gardens and orchards break the monotonous browns of the soil, mountains and mud houses. Some areas in all villages are predominantly comprised of ruins of old houses where people have repatriated.

The inhabitants of Saranan are originally from Kandahar but migrated in the early 1900s to Saripul in northern Afghanistan due to drought and famine, as well as lack of agricultural land (Tapper 1991: 68-75). The population is 32,120 and chiefly Pushtoon Isakzai and sub-tribe Maduzai (Mercy Corps Census 1999).

The population of Surkhab is from the Kandahar area and other provinces of the south. The population of 28,872 is heterogeneous. There are Baluch *kuchis*, nomads, and the following Pushtoon tribes in Surkhab: Mulakhel (Uruzgan), Andar (Ghazni), Wardaki, Barakzai, Alizai, Alokozai, Popolzai, Sulemankhel, Terin, Sayed, Noorzai, Kakar, and Kharoti.

Pir Alizai has a population of 32,254 refugees from Kandahar and Helmand provinces and a few families from the northern areas of

Afghanistan (Mercy Corps Census 1999). Tribally, these Pushtoon are Barakzai, Alizai, Achekzai, Popolzai, Alokozai, Kharoti and Taraki. Both Surkhab and Pir Alizai initially also had Uzbeks, Tajiks and Hazaras but most of these people have moved to urban areas over the last ten years.

Mercy Corps operates eight Basic Health Units (BHUs) and a community development programme in the area. Save the Children (US) runs primary schools, non-formal education for women, home based girls' schools, and a Group Guaranteed Loans and Savings (GGLS) programme. United Nations High Commissioner for Refugees (UNHCR) is involved in repatriation.

Chagai District

The Chagai district borders Afghanistan and Iran. Dalbandin, the district town closest to most refugee villages, thrives on smuggled goods from both countries. There are five refugee villages in the Chagai district: Girdi Jungle, Chagai, Legi Karez, Posti, and Amri. The population of this area is estimated to be approximately 145,806 people (PDH Census 1999). The majority are from Helmand as well as Kandahar provinces in Afghanistan. Apart from Posti, all of the refugee villages are located in dry, desert areas. Posti is located in a long narrow valley with a stream. Therefore, it is possible to grow crops and vegetables on the restricted land area to which refugees have access. Most of the population in these villages is Pushtoon: Isakzai, Noorzai, Popolzai, Alokozai, Daftani, Kharoti, Wardaki, and Andar. Posti is home to mostly Afghan Baluch.

The Project Directorate Health (PDH) of the Pakistani government works together with UNHCR and Mercy Corps in these villages in the areas of health care, community development and repatriation. Save the Children (US) is involved in education and Group Guaranteed Loans and Savings (GGLS).

Loralai and Zhob Districts

The refugee villages in Muslimbagh are Malgagai I and IV. These villages are located along the road to Loralai. The population of these villages is 7,342 (PDH census 1999) and they are predominantly Tokhi, Andar or Sulemankhel Pushtoons.

Loralai is an old garrison town established during the British rule. The refugee villages in this district are: Gazgi Minara, Zar Karez I and III, Spaidar, and Katwai. The population of this area is estimated to be 30,488 people (PDH census 1999). These villages are all established in very dry, desert areas. Water is a continuous problem. An irrigation channel cuts through three of the villages but refugees are not allowed to use this water for it belongs to a landowner for the watering of his orchard. Tribal divisions are between Nasir, Kharoti, Taraki, Wardaki, Andar, Uttak (Zabul), Daftani, and Kandahari Kakar Pushtoons.

The Project Directorate Health (PDH), of the Pakistani government, works together with UNHCR and Mercy Corps in these villages in the areas of health care, community development and repatriation. Save the Children (US) is involved in education and Group Guaranteed Loans and Savings (GGLS).

Methods

This research is a combination of semi-structured open-ended interviews, informal discussions, project activities, and participant observation. Dr. Yasmin Hamidi and the author conducted the interviews for this research. Two Community Development Officers of Mercy Corps, Parween and Farahnaz, acted as research assistants in some of the locations. Research initially commenced in Surkhab and Saranan, two refugee villages in Baluchistan, Pakistan, in March 1998. Interviews were carried out in Afghanistan in March–April 1998 and April–July 1999. Informal discussions and contact with the interviewees and other women continued through friendships, various project activities, and surveys. Research in refugee villages of Baluchistan has continued consistently to date.

Initially, an open-ended interview guideline was used. After the preliminary analysis of the data from refugee villages, it was decided that the format of the interview needed precision and more detail. The initial question format was in parts ambiguous and encouraged yes/no answers rather than description. For further research in refugee villages and project areas in Afghanistan, the interview questions were altered to facilitate the gathering of information and to increase information from the women interviewed. The revised interview format was semi-structured with open-ended questions. The data collected focused on female mobility, access to education, health care, income-generation, training needs, sources of information, repatriation, and perceptions of the current situation in Afghanistan. In 1999, a section on land, food security and women's labour was added. The interview formats can be found in Appendix I.

Comparative data on the situation before the war, during the war, and in present-day Afghanistan was obtained by recording women's life history narratives. Reminiscing about the war was difficult for many women. When Niekbakhta (50, G 2) was asked what life was like during the war, her reply was, "Oh don't ask. After a long time now we have peace. I don't want to remember."

"[The war was] very bad. Don't remind me," Wasila (36, G 6).

"Better not ask [about life during the war]. I don't want to remember. We could not leave," Rasto (37, L 4).

"My childhood was only hearing war; the noise of tanks, jets and rockets. Not good. You know how it has been," Bibigula (28, DM 10).

What is not said can be as important as what is verbally expressed. Therefore, silences and reluctance to discuss certain subjects were noted. Collecting life history narratives triggered conversations about relevant concerns of women: regrets, anecdotes, stories, and gossip. These were recorded as valuable information.

It was useful to carry out group interviews as well as individual interviews. There is greater privacy during an individual interview and even very sensitive issues can be broached. However, a value and advantage of group interviews was observing the ways in which women agree or disagree with each other. This gave a fuller view of reality: how differently issues were perceived by different individuals. Liars got caught. It was not rare for women to candidly interrupt one another and tell us that a woman was not being entirely truthful.

In 1998, in Grishk, Nad-i-Ali and Lashkargah, the research staff were driven to the central bazaar of a research area to continue on foot from one compound to the next. Compounds were generally chosen at random in each area of town or different parts of the village and district. In Lashkargah, three women recommended households that should be interviewed. Two women interviewed were relatives. For interviews in more remote areas of the town, village or district, a vehicle was used.

In Garamser, the research staff stayed at the Hazarjuft hospital. A vehicle was used between compounds more frequently because the Taliban *Wulluswal*, the district commissioner, was in town. Female strangers walking on their own may have created a problem.

In Nawsad, we lived with a family within one of the villages of the area, Deh Baloch. This provided the opportunity to observe how relationships are played out, how households are run, and the divisions of labour. It also allowed us to engage in informal conversations and participate in women's activities.

In the refugee villages in Pishin and Killa Abdullah, interviews and participant observation were carried out during day trips from Quetta. In Dalbandin and Loralai districts, each visit was a week long. Visits included participating in various female and male activities and gatherings in homes, as well as the BHU. Meetings, discussions, conflicts and problem solving within communities were also used as research material.

Interviews in Baluchistan and Afghanistan were conducted in homes of women or the compound of a female friend, neighbour or *Mullah*, the religious leader of the community. All interviews were carried out in the local languages of Pushto or Dari. Some were written in English in the field, others were translated and typed in English in Quetta for analysis purposes. All interviews are filed and compiled onto a computer database at the Mercy Corps Pakistan/Afghanistan office in Quetta, Pakistan.

Interviewees

1998

Ninety-eight women were formally interviewed during 1998. Fifty-five interviews were carried out in the refugee villages in Baluchistan and 43 in Afghanistan. These figures do not include the female health committee members of refugee villages who, during their monthly meetings, contributed information for this report, nor does it include the many women who commented on what interviewees were saying while being interviewed.

Twenty-five women were interviewed in Saranan during five group interviews and eight individual interviews. Fifteen interviews were conducted in both Surkhab and Pir Alizai. One interview in Pir Alizai was a group interview. Even during individual interviews, other women around the household commented on what was being said.

In Afghanistan, sixteen women were interviewed in Hazarjuft and sixteen in Grishk, three in Nad-i-Ali, and eight in Lashkargah City. Between six and eight women who were visiting or who live in the same compound as the interviewee, were present at each interview and commented upon and elaborated on what the woman being interviewed said. Thus, in reality the 43 interviews that were carried out represent the views of more than these 43 women.

In Hazarjuft, all the women interviewed were Pushtoon, aged between 15 and 95. Of the 16 women interviewed, nine had returned from Pakistan. In Grishk, four of the 16 women interviewed were Farsi speakers,[16] the rest were Pushtoon. Three of the women were Shia, the rest Sunni Muslims. The women were aged between 18 and 65. In Lashkargah City, two Pushtoon and six Dari speakers were interviewed. Two of the women were Shias, one was Tajik. The youngest woman interviewed was 25 years old and the oldest 70. In Nad-i-Ali, three Pushtoon women were interviewed, two of them were 38 years old and one was 70. Details of intervie-wees are in Appendix III.

1999-2000

In Nawsad, ten interviews were conducted in each of the following five villages: Deh Baloch, Deh Mian, Gena, Jungolak, and Tangi Aulia. An additional 43 women were interviewed in Hazarjuft. Other villages in Garamser were also targeted. Three women were inter-viewed in the village of Deh Zekria, four in Darweshan, nine in Shamalan, one in Kharai, four in Loy, and six in Laki.

All of these 120 women were Pushtoon Sunni Muslims and spoke Pushto as their mother tongue.

Weekly contact was maintained with women in refugee villages throughout 1999 and 2000. A few formal interviews were also car-ried out: three in Chagai, two in Legi Karez and three in Posti. The women in Posti were Afghan Baluch. They spoke Baluchi as their mother tongue but due to living in Pushtoon areas, they understood and spoke some Pushto too. The village *Mullah* helped translate dur-ing the interview. The women in Chagai and Legi Karez were Pushtoon and spoke Pushto. All the women were Sunni Muslims.

The youngest woman interviewed was 17, the oldest 70. The noted ages of women are not necessarily accurate, as many women do not know their age, but they are indicative. When women are quoted in the text, their age and code of the village they live in are stated. This will give the reader an idea of the age of the woman speaking and where she is living. These interviewee details, as well as the marriage age of the women and their household size, can be found in Appendix III.

---

[5] Also known as Pukhtun in the central and north of Afghanistan and the northwest province of Pakistan. Pathan was the name given to this ethnic group by the British.

[6] Decent is traced through the male members of the family and upon marriage women leave their families to reside with their husband's family.

[7] In Islam, sexuality is perceived as the energy of instincts. These instincts in themselves are not divided into bad or good. What is crucial is how these instincts are used. Laws formed to maintain social order determine the context in which the use of instincts is either right or wrong. It is unnecessary for an individual to control sexual desire for the sake of control; instead, it is to be used according to the requirements of religious law. Sexuality is for procreation and as such is permissible only within marriage. Here it serves the purpose of the Muslim order. Illicit intercourse will destroy this order (Mernissi 1987: 27-30). Female dress and mobility are tied to perceptions of female sexuality.

[8] Relations by marriage.

[9] The Quran recognises this change in a woman's status the following way: "Such elderly women as are past the prospect of marriage, there is no blame on them if they lay aside their outer garments, provided they make not a wanton display of their beauty: but it is best for them to be modest," (Quran 24: 60).

[10] One of the contradictions is between Islam and *Pushtoonwali*. Usually in tribal and rural areas it is Pushtoonwali that wins, but among the educated and urban population it is Islam (Boesen 1983, Donnan 1988: 87-110). One good illustration is that of marriage systems. Brideprice is the form of marital payment used among the Pushtoon while Islam prescribes a system of dowry and mehr (divorce compensation). Most urban, wealthy and educated Pushtoon families have dowry and not brideprice.

[11] One jerib of land is 0.2 hectares.

[12] Other tribes recorded in this area are: Ghilzai, Nasir, Shaikhel, Mohammadzai, Waziri, Kakar, Karaish, Dartokhel, Wardaki, Mashikhel, Sulemankhel, Sayed, Safi, Alizai, Hazarkhel, Mumand, Alikhel, Omarkhel, Miyakhel, Andar, Isakzai, Sadat, Hamadzai, Horyakhel, Shinwari and Baretz (Scott 1990: 12, 24, 26).

[13] This work was funded by the US Bureau for Population, Refugees and Migration.

[14] Surveys done in the 1970s also revealed other tribes or ethnic groups in the area. These were Shaikhail, Hazara, Miyakhel, Sulemankhel, Turkmen, Mohammadzai, Daftani, Tajik, Uzbek, Mullakhel, Sayed, Ibrahimkhel, Niyazai, Nasir, Yusufzai, Wardaki, Taraki, Mahikhel, and Molathel (Scott 1980).

[15] A *karez* is a traditional form of irrigation that accesses ground water through a system of wells and underground and surface water channels. If the wells fill with soil during floods or are damaged by the force of water, underground water channels will become blocked and there will be no running water.

[16] All non-Pushtoons are referred to as Farsi speakers by the women interviewed. This means that Tajiks, Uzbeks and Hazaras, for instance, are considered Farsi speakers although they have their own indigenous languages.

— 4 —

Visibility and Mobility

Purdah

Purdah is currently practiced to a lesser or greater degree in the Muslim world according to individual or family practices, age, class, area of inhabitance, ethnicity, economic and social status, and the influence of religious and political powers. It is an element of daily life that affects social life as well as economic, political, matrimonial, and educational issues.

Originally *purdah* was an urban phenomenon. The veil was worn as an indicator of social status and as protection. Urban elites, the land-lord class and women of religious leaders' families took to wearing the veil to distinguish themselves from the masses. In the 1950s and 60s, this began to change in Afghanistan due to increased migration to the cities because of industrialisation and to high-class women's discarding of the veil. In 1959, King Zahir Shah's government announced the voluntary end of *purdah*. Seclusion and the removal of the veil were left up to individual families. However, rural women continued to use the veil when they visited urban areas as a mark of their sophistication. The veil remained a status symbol for rural women and many of the poorer classes. The *burqa* and *chadar* were sought after goals and external signs of respectability. The general perception of a veiled woman in urban areas was that she was either a villager living or visiting the city, or a woman of lower economic standing (Dupree 1990, Ali Majrooh 1989:91, see also Dupree 1984).

Purdah depends on different things at different times, as Bibi Amina (22, HAS 7) explains, "Sometimes it depends on your husband's mentality, sometimes on culture or rules of the government."

Most rural Afghan women begin "to do" *purdah* and wear the *burqa* when moving outside the village when they marry. However, Seema (26, Las 2) said that she began wearing the *burqa* after the Mujahedin came into power. She had worn only the *chadar* prior to this. "[Dress] depends on where you go," Shekira (45, DM 3). The size of the village or town and where one is going affects female dress and mobility. Most villages in rural Afghanistan are organised into kin-oriented areas within which women can move freely.

Among refugees, the practice of *purdah* often initially becomes stricter. It functions as the protection and defense of the family in an environment that is alien and considered more dangerous than home. It demonstrates the agnatic[17] family's social and ethnic identity in a situation where the male Pushtoon cannot demonstrate this through economic and social autonomy (Boesen 1988: 236-37). However, in some cases when refugee men are unable to find work, their insistence on *purdah* becomes less rigid. As one woman put it, "When there is no food on the table, men open the door," (Dupree 1989: 7).

Taliban and Codes of Dress and Behaviour

The words *chadar, dupatta* or *polene* are used to refer to a large shawl that covers the body and head but leaves the face covered to the degree desired by its wearer. *Chadari* or *burqa* is used to refer to the shuttle-cock-shaped garment worn over the head. It has a mesh or net in front of the eyes. The wearer can choose from a loosely-woven net mesh or a tight one with very small holes. The terms *chadar* and *burqa* will be used in this text to determine the type of attire worn by women.

The Taliban has imposed dress codes for men and women in the areas under their rule. In December 1996, the Department for the

Promotion of Virtue and the Prevention of Vice stated the following:

> As the dignity and honour of a Muslim woman is ensured by observing hejab [covering dress] as requested by Shari'a, all honourable sisters are strongly asked to completely observe hejab as recommended by Shari'a. This can be achieved only if our dear sisters wear burqas, because full hejab cannot be achieved by wearing only a chadar. In cases of violation, no one will have the right of complaint. (Marsden 1999:63)

Purdah restrictions are not uniform in Afghanistan. Despite the Taliban influence, in many cases it is still age, marital status, individual families, geographical area, and economic necessity that determine how much room for maneuver a woman has. In Kabul, and the predominantly Pushtoon and Taliban controlled south, it is demanded that women wear the *burqa*. In Herat, for example, the Taliban demand that women cover from head to toe but women are left to choose how to achieve this. In Jalalabad in 1996, women were asked to wear either a *chadar* or *hijab*, a long coat and head scarf (See Le Duc and Sabri 1996: 19-22, Dupree 1998:150-166).

Men's dress code is also strict; all men must wear *shalwar kamiz*, a tunic with wide loose trousers, and preferably a turban. Their head should be covered and they are not allowed to shave or trim their beard. In December 1996, the Taliban announced:

> Since the Prophet, Muhammed, peace be upon him, did not trim his beard all his life, therefore all government employees are hereby informed that they should grow their beards within a month and a half in accordance with the Noble Hadith of the prophet, in order to be regarded as a true Muslim. (Marsden 1999:63)

There is only one visible exception to the rule: the traffic police in Kandahar. These are old men who held this post in pre-war years.

They wear their old western-style white and blue uniform with a peaked cap. Also, Ariana pilots[18] are exempt from wearing a turban and *shalwar kamiz*, but not from an untrimmed beard.

Men are generally mobile with the exception of members of some ethnic groups. The Hazaras, surrounded by predominantly Pushtoon populations, feel restricted to certain areas of the country. In Kandahar and other cities, however, ethnic minorities, mostly Tajiks and Uzbeks, are represented in the labour force and can be seen moving around the city. Since late 1999, however, restrictions on the movements of Hazaras have grown strict within Afghanistan. They have been stopped before they reach Kandahar, searched, and sent back to the districts they traditionally populate.

Women are quick to point out that the government-imposed restrictions impact men as well as women. In many households, family income has been reduced due to the restriction of women working outside the home. The workload of men has increased. In areas where women have had tasks outside the home, these now fall on the shoulders of the men.

"[The Taliban has placed] restrictions. They are problems but not only for women, also for men," Bibi Ayesha (32, SAR 5).

"Negative changes are war, no education and too many restrictions for all men and women," Marzia (50, GRI 12).

Rural Versus Urban Areas

There have always been differences in the mobility and dress of women in rural and urban areas. These differences have to do with the culture, security and the level of education in an area. The Taliban have enforced a unified dress code for all. Some women feel that this has had little difference to life in the village while others point our how much stricter observances have become in the urban areas.

"[We have restrictions] because of our culture and tradition in the village. In Afghanistan you can see different cultures in the city and rural areas," Azmat (30, HAZ 22).

"[Life] is the same in the village but in the city it is more difficult now. Life in the village and life in the city are very different. [Purdah] is strict in our culture in the village . . . [I wore] a *burqa* when I was young or when I go out of the village, a *chadar* now," Nadia (40, HAZ 35).

"The situation is very bad. Everybody says no rights for women, but even before the war we had the same condition for women in the village. [What is] different from before is that restrictions are for women in the cities too," Nadira (52, SAR 10).

The differences in dress and mobility in the urban and rural environment are best illustrated by young women who were brought up in cities such as Kabul, Kandahar or Lashkargah and have since moved to the rural areas, usually as a result of marriage. These women benefited from at least primary education and feel the restrictions of the Taliban far more than women who never attended school or had relative freedom of movement.

Saliqa (19, HAZ 27) was born in Hazarjuft but brought up in Lashkargah. After her marriage a year ago, she moved back to Hazarjuft. "I had a good life [in Lashkargah] going to school. Schools closed when Talibs came. Peace but no life. I'm six months pregnant. Now it is fine. I'm happy with my husband. [Mobility] is worse now because of the Taliban."

"I was born in Khost and brought up in Kabul, then came to Hazarjuft. When I was a child I had a good life. Being in school was really nice, but after the Talibs came, everything changed. I married when I was 16. After one year [I delivered a son]. Now I am happy and busy with my son. . . . In the village [restrictions] are because of the culture and religion. . . . Now I wear *burqa*, before nothing," Pargula (18, HAZ 25).

"Restrictions are the same here [Hazarjuft] but in Laghman we had less restrictions. Here [I wear] *chadar* inside the village, out of the village *burqa*, but before just *chadar*," Qandigul (36, HAZ 32).

Qandi (45, DM 4) is originally from Kandahar but has lived in Nawsad since her marriage 35 years ago. She says that she travels to

Kandahar and other areas with some male member of the family because life in the village is boring. She says that since the Taliban, things have changed in the city but not in the village. "It is the same here [in Nawsad] but in Kandahar it is more difficult than before," Qandi (45, DM 4).

In Nawsad, women travel inside the village. Sometimes they go with children or alone. In villages, one rarely sees women wearing the *burqa*. Women in Nawsad were upset that Afghan Mercy Corps' female research staff were wearing a *burqa*. They said it was unnecessary within the village.[19] Women travelling outside their village often wear a *burqa*, particularly if they are travelling far and are young. Older women wear a *chadar*. If they travel outside the village they usually go to Grishk, Marja, Lashkargah, or Kandahar.

When asked why restrictions are placed on women, Kobra (17, DB 9) answered simply, "This is our culture – Nawsad culture." She has traveled outside of Nawsad all the way to Pakistan and acknowledges that life is different for women elsewhere. In Laki, women move around in the village wearing only a *chadar*. The only *burqa*-clad woman in the village we saw was the female medical officer of the Mercy Corps BHU. She explained it was easier for her to wear a *burqa* as her dress is more modern and she is an outsider in the village. Inside the village, women, including the medical officer, move around alone. If they venture outside the village, a son or grandchild will most often accompany them. Women say they will wear a *burqa* if they travel far out of the village such as to Marja or Lashkargah. But even this is not uniform.

"Out of the village I go with *burqa*, but look at my neighbour, she is with *chadar*," Guldana (19, L 6).

For most rural women, the Taliban are only one in the succession of governments they have had over the years. Nafasa (28, HAS 9) mentions that the restriction are due to the Taliban and culture and that the restrictions are more than before. In Garamser, the restrictions seem to be a combination of various things. Nobody says restrictions are due only to the Taliban.

"[As I grew older] different kinds of governments – communist, Mujahedin, Taliban – war and peace," Gulsima (25, HAZ 56).

"[Restrictions] are because of the family, culture and government," Kemia Gula (24, HAZ 23).

"If I go far, then I wear *burqa*, otherwise a big *chadar* is enough," Azmat (30, HAZ 22).

"[The situation is like this because of] culture, government and illiteracy," Dawlat (52, HAZ 37).

In Kandahar, all young women were wearing a *burqa*. Older women were only wearing a *chadar* with their face completely uncovered. They can also be seen in the bazaar areas and talking with male shopkeepers. In Grishk and Lashkargah, women wore *burqas* and older women wearing just *chadars* walked in the streets. In Lashkargah, restrictions on women's mobility and visibility began with the Mujahedin in 1992. Women had enjoyed relative freedoms prior to this.

A member of Mercy Corps' international staff, who in early 2000 travelled from Masood-controlled northern Afghanistan to Kandahar in the space of a week, commented on how surprised he was to find women more covered up in Masood areas than in Taliban heartland in Kandahar. He said he saw many more female faces in the streets of Kandahar than in the non-Taliban north.

Punishments regarding inappropriate dress are rumoured about, but very few in the south who were spoken to have been subject to any disciplinary action in this regard. In the few cases that women had heard of someone being reprimanded by the Taliban's Department for the Promotion of Virtue and the Prevention of Vice, it was the male relatives of a woman not deemed appropriately dressed who were punished, not the woman herself.

Women express their resistance to certain edicts of the Taliban in their everyday lives. In public spaces, one can observe women "bending the rules." Walking around the village, women pull the *chadar* in front of their face only when passing a stranger or *Talib*, and as soon as they have passed they relax their *purdah*. This is also true in cities. In Kandahar, we observed women moving around the city. In quiet residential streets they lift the front of their *burqa* up onto their head. It is pulled down quickly as soon as a man, a Taliban vehicle or Taliban post is seen. Indeed, we learned to adhere to restrictions the same way, covering our faces only when Talibs were around, passing Taliban vehicles, posts, or the buildings of the Taliban's Department for the Promotion of Virtue and the Prevention of Vice.

Photography was one way women felt they could get something of their own back. One woman in Nawsad asked me into her bedroom and told me to photograph her quickly before anyone came into the room. Another woman at the Laki BHU boldly placed herself in front of my camera and said, "Sister, photograph me all you like." Then she threw her head back and laughed, "The Taliban don't like this!"

Age

Among the Pushtoon, insistence on *purdah* relaxes as a woman grows older. After menopause a woman is no longer as great a threat to the family honour and she has earned the respect accorded to an older woman. Under the rule of Taliban it is the older women who are least restricted.

"Because of my age it is easier now [to move around]. It is in our culture and religion that young women should have strict *purdah*," Khora (53, DZ 3).

The same restrictions on dress and mobility do not apply to older women the same way as to young women of reproductive age. As 70-year-old Bibigul (Las I) explains,

"I use *dupatta*,[20] but in the war and before the war I wore *burqa*. We are allowed to go out everywhere but only old women can go shopping, otherwise there is no problem to get out. Not to the fields here but in the villages it is possible. I can go anywhere. I go to relatives' houses, neighbours . . . I go to other districts like Grishk, Kandahar, Iran, and Pakistan anytime I want. ... I can go alone inside the city but to Iran with a female and to Pakistan with a male. . . . It was easier [to move around when I was younger] but it was not good in our culture to move alone but now I am old I can move alone. Now, young women can't travel alone from one village to another village, but inside the city or village it is not a problem . . . . It is because of the situation and also culture, but I don't know why they don't allow young women to do shopping. You can cross the bazaar but not do shopping."

This is echoed by 95-year-old Rangina (HAZ 7) in Hazarjuft, "I'm too old. I'm not under Taliban policy." And 65-year-old Hoor (GRI 3) in Grishk, "My life now it is OK. I'm too old and I'm not under the restriction of the Taliban. I hope that peace is lasting because I am tired of war."

"If you are old like me, [there is] no attraction so it is easy to move around now. . . . Now I am waiting for the graveyard," Khaldara (62, HAZ 28).

"I don't travel often anymore. If it is an urgent issue, then travel . . . In the village, of course, [I move around] alone, but out of the village I can't go alone because I am old and I can't find my way. Now [mobility] is easier because I am old. In our culture ladies can't go alone . . . I think it is because of our culture and tradition. When I was young up until the age of 45, I had a *burqa*, but now *chadar*," Badro (60, TA 1).

"I am [allowed to go out] because I am old. The restrictions are not because of the Taliban, it is because of our culture," Shakar (60, G 10).

With age, the insistence to wear a *burqa* decreases. Rasto (37, L 4) explained that she wore a *burqa* for ten years after her marriage, and since then has used only a *chadar*. Other women express having the same experience.

"When I was young I was wearing *burqa* but now a big *chadar*," Bibi Ayesha (40, G 1).

"When I was young and when I go out of the village [I wear] *burqa*, but now just *chadar*," Badro (41, L 2).

"When I was young [I wore] *burqa*, since 25 years just a *chadar*," Sahiba (60, L I).

"When I was 20, I was wearing a *burqa* but now just a *chadar*," Koko (62, HAS 6).

The laxing of the rules for older women is also expressed by women in the refugee villages. Some feel they will be able to work in the fields as well as do other labour work outside the home in Afghanistan, whereas, others clearly state that any work they do will be restricted to their compound.

Women Alone

Widows usually live with their in-laws or return to live with their own parents. Very few widows in the south live on their own. The father, brother-in-law, brother, or son of the woman is responsible for her protection, and so she must seek his permission for travel and moving outside the compound.

"Now life is good but I am a widow and have only one son who is 14 years old. A widow has no life. I can't go out much. My brother-in-law does not allow me. If I go, it is once a year to my brother's house with the children. This is not because of the situation, it is because men are very religious," Sabira (43, DB I).

"Life of a widow. What do you think it is like? I am young and I can't decide for myself. Women have no life. At the parents' house, there are restrictions from the brother and father. In the in-laws' house, the husband, and if you are a widow then your son too puts restrictions on you," Bibi Nazamin (30, TA 7).

Those women who are separated from their husbands, or who have been left by their husbands, face many difficulties if the husband does not take financial responsibility for her. In such cases, the woman's mobility might not be curbed but she relies heavily on the charity of those around her.

"My husband is living with other wives and doesn't give me food, money. I'm asking other people to give me something for my children," Sherin (48, DB 2).

Zargara (40, HAZ 49) divorced her first husband after seven years of marriage, at the age of 19, after he took a second wife. She was remarried to another man as his second wife. After bearing him three children, his first wife kicked her out of the house. She now works in other people's houses cleaning, washing clothes and making bread.

Khor Bibi (18, HAS 5) has been left in her father's house by her husband. She says that in her father's house she has freedom to visit whom she likes, when she likes, clad in only a *chadar*. She comments that, "A good life is only for the men who have the right of decision making."

Roshana (35, HAZ 50) also lives with her parents despite being married at the age of nine. After the *nikah*,[21] her husband went to study in Kabul. While he was away, her family fled to Pakistan as refugees. They stayed for 11 years. In the meantime, he married an educated woman in Kabul. Roshana met her husband again in 1999. Her husband now divides his time between his second wife in Kabul and Roshana in Hazarjuft.

Women whose husbands have more than one wife complain about life being difficult, as resources have to be shared between more people. The husband may be stricter with one wife than another. When a man dies, his wives become responsible for taking care of each other and all offspring.

"I am the third wife of my husband. Now he is dead and we have a very difficult life. My sons work in others' fields and one is a *Talib*," Hussungula (44, DB 8).

"My husband has a second wife, so life has become more difficult. Sharing a husband is very difficult to tolerate," Guldasta (58, TA 4).

Social Class and Wealth

Social class and wealth play a role in dress and mobility. The women of *khans*, big landlords or important elders, do not adhere as strictly to the dress code. Their status protects them from being harassed.

This was also evident when taking photographs. Women were generally very open to being photographed, but their men would not give permission. The wealthy and women of important men let me photograph them freely. They said they didn't need to ask for permission and if people found out they would not dare complain. One woman in the Laki BHU responded, "We are *Khans* in Safar, yes you can take a picture of me."

Wealth, often from poppy, has enabled families to travel more frequently and travel farther. Travel to Kandahar or Pakistan even to Saudi Arabia for Haj,[22] has increased. Both men and women from rural Afghanistan are travelling for Haj.

Purchasing vehicles has made entire families more mobile. Increased mobility has resulted in better access to health care for people living in remote areas. However, in the majority of the country the lack of adequate transportation and poor road conditions are still a problem. "My husband has a second wife. [He] is busy with poppy. . . I just go to my mother's house. I go with my husband. Now that we have a car it is easier to move," Bibi Gul (32, DB 7).

Livelihood and Ethnicity

Generally, women in southern Afghanistan seem to be going about their daily business outside the home. Very few women work in the fields, but they are involved in later stages of the production or processing of crops. This is the traditional division of labour in the majority of the villages. However, along the road between Grishk and Hazarjuft, some women were wearing only a *chadar* while at work in the fields. One woman in Nad-i-Ali whose family grows poppy and works in the fields with her husband.

Women with their faces uncovered can be seen washing clothes along the banks of the Boghra canal in Helmand, or carrying containers of water back to the house. Children, boys and girls, swim in the canal while animals graze along the banks.

Hazara men and women do not adhere as strictly to *purdah*. Men and women work closely together in agricultural production. Even male strangers are able to see and talk to Hazara women.

Kuchi women nomads are unaffected by the edicts of the Taliban. They continue their seasonal migration as they have always done. They move with their caravan of camels, goats and dogs dressed in colourful, heavy, embroidered dresses worn with *shalwars*, trousers, made of five yards of cloth, their head covered loosely by a *chadar*.

In the spring of 2000, the beginning of a drought affected the seasonal travel of the Kuchi people. Their livestock – livelihood were dying due to the lack of water and grazing. The Taliban moved some of these people and their animals in "borrowed" trucks to Herat, while others looked for grazing lands in areas they normally do not travel in.

Shopping

In Nawsad, shopping has never been something women do. Bazaars are generally far from home compounds and shopping is seen as the responsibility and the duty of men, not women. In southern Helmand, particularly in the more urban areas, some women were accustomed to shopping prior to the rule of the Taliban.

Under the Taliban, women in Lashkargah are not allowed to shop alone because this involves contact with shopkeepers: men. If women go shopping they have to stand away from the shop in the street while their husband brings them the merchandise for their approval.

"We are allowed to go out everywhere but only old women can do shopping. Other than that it is no problem to go out. It's not possible to go to the fields here, but in the villages it is possible. I go to relatives' houses, neighbours," Bibigul (70, LAS I).

"I, or we, are allowed to go out of the compound anywhere in our city, but we can't do shopping. In the city when we visit friends or relatives' houses, it is no problem. It is not necessary to have male company. If we travel to another city or village we have to be with a male," Bibi Gouhar (45, LAS 3).

In Nad-i-Ali, restrictions on shopping preceded the enforcement by the Taliban.

"I'm only allowed to visit neighbours, not shop. It is a very small village so women are not going shopping. It is not only because of the Taliban but also because of our culture," Shoogufa (38, NAD 1).

In Garamser, the restriction on women shopping is not as absolute but women feel it is better to refrain from it.

"I'm allowed to go to others' houses. Only shopping is difficult. Some of the Taliban are kind but some are very serious, so better not go," Hazrata (55, HAZ 10).

"I'm allowed to go out of the home, for shopping it is sometimes difficult. The Taliban don't allow us but some of them are good. . . . When I was young, I could not go alone because I could not find the way . . . also in our culture it was bad if young women went out. It is easy for me now," Gulaba (48, HAZ 3).

"The [bazaar] is not too close, but women can't go. First, it is not our duty. Secondly, there is pressure from husbands and the Taliban," Walat Bibi (19, HAS 4).

"We women don't do shopping, it is not in our culture," Kheshmesh (70, DA 2).

"I am allowed [to move around] except to go shopping. It is not good for a woman, especially a young woman to go shopping," Bibi Borjana (30, DA 4).

For some women like Khadija (42, HAZ 1) the restrictions on shopping have made little impact. "Life is easier than before the Taliban, only women can't do shopping alone. But I never went shopping. My husband or others have always brought me the things I want because I felt scared. Before we used the *burqa* too and now also. It is not because of the situation. We do this because of our culture and tradition."

In Laki, women do not shop. There is no central bazaar area. Women say that everything they need is available but it is not close by. In Grishk, women are permitted by the Taliban to shop on their own, interact with shopkeepers, and move around the town visiting women in other compounds, provided they wear the *burqa*. Even so, the Taliban interfere. "It was easy to move around before. Nobody asked where you were going, but the Taliban interfere with everything," Shahgul (52, GRI 1).

In the village of Gena in Nawsad, Niekbakhta (50, G 2) explains, "Yes, there are [bazaars] but men do the shopping because it is not too close by." There are exemptions to the rules. Bibi Noor (50, DM 5) says that she will not go shopping regularly but, "I go if there is no man at home."

Mobility and Mahram

Women are permitted to visit relatives, neighbours and friends on their own within their home city or town. If they travel to locations outside the city they should be accompanied by *mahram*, a close male relative, such as their husband, son, father, brother, or the *Mullah*. The *Mullah* of the area in which a family resides is permitted to see and talk to the women of his "congregation," as Badra (41, L 2) explains, "[I talk] to everybody in the family, to the *Mullah* and to women in the village."

Travel accompanied by a *mahram* is not always due to restrictions. Some women are inexperienced and frightened to travel on their own. Few women know their way around outside the village.

"When I know the way, I travel or go alone or with female company, but if I don't [know the way] I need male company," Khadija (42, HAZ 1).

"Access to health care in a village is not easy because there is no hospital. So if a woman from a village travels to a city or district, how can she go alone because a village woman does not know the way and they don't have the courage to travel alone," Halima (46, SAR 4).

"[If I go] far I travel with male company. It is not because of the Taliban, but the reason is that we don't have the courage. . . . [Travel is] easier now because of transportation," Niekbakhta (50, G 2).

"I don't have the courage to go out alone in the village, so for me going alone or with someone makes no difference," Shabnam (42, DM 6).

"Whenever I want to, I can go out. But I don't go out of the village alone because I can't find my way," Koko (62, HAS 6).

Between villages and even in cities like Grishk and Lashkargah, a favoured mode of female transportation is the donkey. Women ride on their own and occasionally one sees two donkeys, facing different directions, "parked" while their riders chat. These women are either wearing a *burqa* or a *chadar*.

Only women travelling between cities or far from their villages are accompanied by an adult male *mahram*. In the cities, some women walk alone and some are accompanied by children, very few with a grown up male relative.

"I travel more inside Nawsad. I go to the nearest places with children or other females but further with my husband . . . now we can travel in a car. Before it was very difficult . . . you can move easily and you can save time. . . . For us, 30 years ago was the same restrictions, and now too," Bibi Ayesha (40, G I).

"Our Men" and Talibs

It is evident from women's narratives that mobility within the villages, and even urban areas to some extent, depends on the men of the family, not necessarily the Taliban.

"[Restrictions] are because of our men; brother, father, son, and husband," Shamsa (40, G 7).

Kheshmesh (70, DA 2) characterised her life the following way: "I was born and brought up in Darweshan. My life was good; we had good food, enjoyment and peace. I got married, had children, then listened to my husband all the time, war, peace."

Women, particularly in north Helmand, say that for as long as they can remember, they have had to have permission from their husbands to leave their own compound. In Nawsad, one woman who had gone to visit her sick sister-in-law, was suffering the consequences of not asking for permission from her husband. He had refused to sleep with her for the past three months and forbade her to leave the compound even to attend a family member's engagement party.

Torpakey (32, GRI 10) is not allowed outside of her compound, even to visit relatives without her husband. Eighteen-year-old Shafiqa (GRI 15) explains that her mobility depends on her husband's mood. Being young doesn't help either, she adds. Kandi (40) in Dehmian, Nawsad, agrees. "All things are up to the mood of the husband. If his mood is good, he will give permission and take you wherever. If he is in a bad mood, you can be dying and he won't take you anywhere."

Life has changed little for many of these rural women under Taliban restrictions. Before the war, Bibi Amina (45 SUR 6) points out, "Our men were like the Taliban but that time there was no problem from government."

"Restriction on mobility is not from now. We had it from before, but now it has come on paper. Even if the Talibs allow us to go out, our men do not allow us. And another reason is education. We cannot read or write so we are blind. That is why we cannot be mobile," Amina (38, TA 2).

"Before, the pressure was just from inside the house. Now it is from outside too. I mean the government," Babo (28, HAS 8).

"I know Taliban put some rules but before we had the same life. Only the direction of instruction has changed," Bibigula (55, HAZ 4).

"We have restrictions from culture, which we call the male side and restrictions from the government," Gulsima (25, HAZ 56).

"Of course, life is sometimes difficult but no different for us. The problems are only for educated women and women who have no male company [widows] or women who want to work and get education. . . . We are comfortable with this life, no difference for us. The Taliban is no problem for us," Bibi Hawa (49, SAR 6).

"We had restrictions only from our men, now we have both from our men and Taliban," Bibi Borjana (30, DA 4).

"It is the same. My mother had the same life," Shafiqa (20, DM 7).

Echoing the above sentiments, one woman told Dr. Yasmin, "Don't worry about us. We had the same restrictions before. Worry about yourself, Kabuli woman. You cannot work."

Security

There is general acknowledgement among men and women, whatever their views on the Taliban, that the Taliban has managed to provide what no other regime has been able to over the past two decades: security. Some call it peace; others feel peace is still too optimistic a term.

During the war, women were relatively unrestricted by the government, but there was no security. Rural women agree that the worst time for them was during the Russian occupation and the Mujahedin. The Taliban have disarmed the population. Women say that during the rule of the Taliban violence, stealing and looting has decreased and women are safer particularly from incidences of sexual violence.

"During Najib we had problems, not like the times of the Mujahedin, they were worse. Now we have peace and a safe life. New people, projects, more communications with other villages. Peace. No war," Sabira (43, DB 1).

"It is good now. During the war there were lots of violations against women," Badamgul (35, HAZ 57).

"First we wanted peace. Now we have it. Before the Taliban, women and girls were under sexual violence. We were powerless. Their [Mujahedin's] language was the gun and killing people," Khadija (42, HAZ 1).

"Village life is not good – no electricity, no life, no school. No change, just instead of war, we have peace . . no visible change, the same life . . . [during the war] life was very bad, insecure, especially for women," Khayato (44, DB 10).

"I had the same life as my children have. No education but peace was at least for a few years. I enjoyed my childhood . . . [I was] married when I was seven . . . in my in-laws house – awful. . . . War took place. All of us were displaced and moved to the mountains. There was no food and a lot of problems. [Life was] full of violence. Sexual violence was also visible. . . . Now it is OK. I enjoy life. After a long time, we live with peace and are back on our land," Shahwazira (37, TA 3).

"We had a very bad life. The Taliban brought peace," Nasrin (30, J 5).

"The war was very bad. No human rights," Bibi Borjana (30, DA 4).

"[Life during the war] was very bad – sexual abuse of women . . . now it is OK. At least my children are alive. I enjoy living with them," Wasila (40, J 10).

"[During the war] life was strange. No security. When you don't have peace, you don't have life," Ram Bibi (59, DM 2).

"[The war] was the worst era of my life. Life was full of violence . . . [now] peace, temporary. But I hope it could be stable peace," Wasila (25, TA 6).

"Now it is OK. We have peace and my husband works," Walat Bibi (19, HAS 4).

"Peace is with us. . . . Now it is fine, not bad life. Peace," Rasto (37, L 4).

"This is the first time in my life that I have seen peace. This is a change," Gulghotai (20, DM 1).

"My life is very good. We have peace and live in a place free of fighting," Bibi Noor (50, DM 5).

"I am a rural woman. This life is more than what I want. There is no war and life is with peace. We want such life without war and poverty," Shabnam (42, DM 6).

The fears and reality of war is recent. There are those who are less optimistic about the chance that the current peace will last.

"Peace, this is a change. But still peace is not forever. We fear that war will start again. . . . Our children have peace but no education," Zargula (21, L 3).

"[My children] have had no access to education, [they have had] an insecure life. They still think they will be taken to war by the government of the Taliban," Nadia (40, HAZ 35).

"We had no responsibility when we were children, but our children have lots of responsibility and they live with fear," Bibi Hazrat (50, HAZ 45).

"I was born in Darweshan and brought up here as well. Also, I was 15 years in Pakistan. My childhood was not bad but war and moving to Pakistan was not good . . . . [Recently] there are many changes; reconstruction of our village, peace, more awareness, good transportation . . . my life, it is OK, not many problems, but I still wait for another war. Maybe again we have to move to another place," Bibi Borjana (30, DA 4).

---

[17] Male line of family.

[18] Ariana is the Afghan airline.

[19] In 1998, the Afghan research staff wore *burqas* in the field. In 1999, Dr. Yasmin traveled wearing a *burqa* or just a *chadar*.

[20] Dupatta in this context is the same as *chadar*, a large cotton, wool or thin polyester shawl.

[21] The official marriage contract.

[22] Pilgrimage to Mecca in Saudi Arabia.

— 5 —

Social Animals

Women's Activities

Women gather together for a number of activities, celebrations and life ceremonies: engagements, weddings, funerals, circumcisions, naming ceremonies and birthdays. *Eid*[23] celebrations are other formal activities during which women interact. In addition, much informal visiting takes place between women in all the research areas. A few women, usually young brides, are not permitted to visit relatives, friends or neighbours alone.

"[I talk] to every woman and some men who are relatives because we are social animals," Niekbakhta (50, G 2).

When together, women talk, display new clothes, sing, dance, tell stories, cry, encourage and assure one another, backstab and "backbite," especially their daughter-in-laws (Sakina, GRI 4), and recite the Quran. *Talawat-e-Quran*, a group recitation out loud, is most common when condoling the loss of a family member. Silent reading of the Quran, *Khatme Quran*, is also done in a group by women.

Older women watch what younger women do and they are important in maintaining the social history of their family, area and population. "We old people recall our youth and talk about it, we sing and dance," Sahiba (60, L I).

In Nawsad, the edict that has most angered women has been restrictions on listening to secular music and thus singing and dancing. Singing and music is a central part of Pushtoon women's self-expression (Grima 1993). Fifty-year-old Gul Bibi in Tangi Aulia,

Nawsad, treated me to a performance of the history of her village and life as she started to sing during our conversation, "We will be burned by our poverty . . . ."

In Nawsad, Shamsa (40, G 7) and Shabnam (42, DM 6), say that they get together less with other women now during the Taliban regime than before. Shabnam said that in Deh Mian, Nawsad, they used to have a spring *mela*,[24] but not anymore. Bibi Ayesha (40, G I) says that they sing less too, but Shamsa says that singing and dancing are still reasons for which women get together. In one village, a large portable stereo stood in the corner of the room beside the sewing machine. Both were in good use.

Women also get together for doing household work. They clean, cook and eat together, help each other to organise parties or to make up and dress the bride. At harvest, they help each other with picking and drying the fruit and cleaning crops. Sewing and washing clothes is often done together. Along the Boghra canal, women can be observed washing clothes. In the refugee village, Surkhab, a wall has been built across the *godar*[25] where women wash clothes and come to get the water. Men say that they are not allowed in the *godar*, but admit that they do go sometimes and try and get a glimpse of women; particularly young men who are looking for a bride. In some villages along the Boghra, a makeshift wall has been erected in the water to hide the *godar* from male view.

The village Basic Health Unit (BHU) is an important meeting place for women. In the refugee villages women have formed health management committees. The main committees meet regularly at the BHU with Mercy Corps staff for health awareness training and problem solving. Here they are also able to meet visitors of their village.

Women's Sources of Information

Women's life history narratives demonstrate the many ways in which these communities have changed and how rural women themselves have become aware of their position and rights. Afghan women never had to fight for their rights. Male leaders announced the voluntary end of seclusion in 1959, and the constitution gave women the vote and the right to education and work (Dupree 1984). Now, male leaders have taken those rights away. What is ironic, is that the emergence of the Taliban and the world's reaction to their edicts have contributed to the increased awareness that rural women have of their position and rights.

"Things have changed a lot: roads, television, airplane, cars. . . . When I was a child we traveled on donkeys but now we travel in cars. Now I can hear from BBC radio that women are also part of society and they also have rights," Gulaba (48, HAZ 3).

"I never knew what politics was, now everybody talks about political issues and groups," Rahmato (35, HAZ 11).

"Women in the village had no value when we were children, we were unaware of our nature, who we are. When we got married we just worked like servants and gave birth, no rights. Before, I thought all women in the world are like me, but now I am aware that all women are not the same," Roqia (38, HAZ 9).

"Too much change. Everything is destroyed. Love gave its place to hate and fighting. Another change is that new machinery came: planes, cars, telephones in the villages, TV . . . people are becoming aware of their rights. They are not slaves anymore," Hazrata (55, HAZ 10).

Women's sources of information are predominantly BBC radio, their male relatives, and other women they meet. The importance of radio has increased in Afghanistan since the Taliban have banned televisions and secular music: listening to instrumental music and love songs.

"We are not allowed to watch TV. They [Taliban] inspect, so we sold it," Shahgul (52, GRI 1).

The BBC broadcasts programmes both in Pushto and Dari twice a day. On Fridays, there are three broadcasts. These broadcasts include news bulletins, educational dramas, health information, interviews, announcements, sports, and answering letters of people looking for lost relatives. A long standing favourite is the educational drama series "New Life, New Home."

In Tangi Aulia, Nawsad, Bibigula (38, TA 5) explains, "We get awareness through radio and even you are here. This is the first time that women from outside have come to our village and that is change." Three women in the refugee villages mentioned relatives as important sources of information, another mentioned letters. The Mullah was also mentioned as a source of information. Illiterate women, both refugees and those in Afghanistan, rely on verbal messages sent via children, their husbands or relatives. A significant centre for the circulation of information is the village BHU. Women pass on information and gossip about what they have heard when they meet with each other at the BHU. Community health workers also act as important sources of information.

"Here we have a BHU, with all the staff, we have FCHWs [Female Community Health Workers] now, but we have in the camp or this village, the families of Taliban and they come here sometimes, but they don't tell us anything. But inside Afghanistan we hear about [the situation] but I don't know how much of it is true because we people make very big things from small things. This is our habit," Delbar (43, SAR 7).

Children are an integral part in women's networking. "Children are our right hand," says Rangina (95, HAZ 7). All of the interviewed women said that they use children as messengers, not only to other women and relations, but also to their husbands. As young boys often have few restrictions on their mobility and visibility, they can be important sources of information for women.

---

[23] Muslim religious celebration.
[24] *Mela* refers to a market or festival.
[25] Place where women collect water. In Surkhab, it is an irrigation channel.

— 6 —

Health Care

Southern Helmand

Access to health care has always been poor in the rural areas of Helmand province. In Hazarjuft, there was only a trained nurse who was approached if home remedies did not work until Mercy Corps re-opened the Hazarjuft hospital in December 1998 and four Basic Health Units (BHUs); one in Mianpushta and Laki each in 1999, and one in Safar and Benader in 2000.[26] The Hazarjuft hospital had originally been built by Americans and destroyed by war. Prior to the opening of the hospital and BHUs, people traveled far for health services. Lashkargah and Grishk have private clinics and hospitals, but more serious cases were referred to Kandahar, Kabul or Pakistan.

Both the hospital and BHUs have male and female medical doctors, since, according to the Taliban, women should be treated by female doctors. However, some members of these communities believe the skills of the male medical officers to be more reliable and will thus, try and bring their wives or daughters to be treated by the male doctor. Patients pay Afs.9000[27] for a consultation with the doctor and the full price for medicines. This has proven to be affordable and it enables the services to be partly self-sustaining.

No woman interviewed in Garamser is barred access to health care. Even unmarried women, such as Wolles Bibi (25, HAS I), who is not allowed to go visiting outside her home compound is allowed to go to the hospital when she needs to. All women interviewed had heard of the hospital or BHUs even if they personally had not needed to see a doctor.

Women say that the hospital and BHUs have solved the problem of having to travel far for health care. This has cut down much of the expenses previously involved in travel for medical attention.

"The hospital is not close but it is much better than going to Lashkargah," Zargara (70, HAZ 38). This is echoed by Shahperai (50, HAZ 58), "[The hospital] is not close but still much better than having to go to Lashkargah. [We have] good results of the treatment and everybody has access."

"[The hospital] is not close but we have access. . . . . Now we don't have to travel far," Zaiba (70, HAZ 51).

"[The hospital] is not too close . . . it is good even for the poor," Jawahir (45, HAZ 53).

"Yes, here is a [hospital]. It is not close – one-hour walk. All [health] services are available," Shah Bibi (45, HAZ 54).

Women are particularly pleased with having access to health care around the clock and being able to have all health services – open patient department, laboratory, X-ray, immunisation, delivery room – all under one roof.

"We can get all services in one place," Gulsima (25, HAZ 56).

Those who have repatriated feel the services offered to be much better than they had access to in refugee villages in Pakistan.

"There is not much difference [between Hazarjuft and the refugee village] on the home level but here it is better for any complications. We have a hospital but [in Pakistan] there was no hospital . . . I would like to work as a traditional birth attendant in the village . . . the hospital and bridge are the best help for the people in the village," Bibi Hazrat (50, HAZ 45).

Informal discussions were held with 15 women who had come to the Laki BHU for medical care one July morning. Before the BHU was built, women travelled far for health services, usually to Lashkargah or Kandahar and, once it opened, to the Hazarjuft hospital. Economically the BHU has had a great impact on the community. Previously going to see a doctor was very expensive: travel costs, food and lodging, as well as consultation fees and medicine. More specifically for women, access to health services has improved great-ly as they are able to come to the BHU on their own, without a *mahram*, often leaving their children at home sleeping or under the watchful eye of a neighbour or older sibling. Thirty-five-year-old Hadija says, "I put my child to sleep at home, come to the BHU, go back – the child is still sleeping."

Previously, women in Laki would only be taken to see a doctor in an emergency or when their condition became very serious. This was due to the distance to the hospital. A trip to the doctor meant at least one day of lost labour for the husband, as he had to accompany her. Men were therefore reluctant to take women for health care unless it became absolutely necessary. Women also mentioned that having a health facility close by means that their children don't suffer as much. It was difficult to take children to see a doctor. Also if the mother had to go it meant having to travel not only with her husband because she didn't know the way to the city where the health facility was located, but she had to take her brood with her also.

The Laki BHU drew people from Safar and Benader before BHUs were built there. Men and women from these areas mentioned how much cheaper and easier it is for them to travel to Laki instead of having to travel all the way to Hazarjuft or even farther to Lashkargah or Kandahar. From Safar to Laki and back costs an aver-age of Afs.10 000,[28] while a round trip to Lashkargah costs Afs.200 000.[29]

Northern Helmand

There is only one clinic run by an Afghan non-governmental organ-ization (NGO) in Nawsad's central bazaar, Absina Mother Child Health Clinic. The staff consists of a male medical officer, his wife who is a nurse, and his sisters who act as pharmacist and health edu-cator. The doctor and his family left Kabul because "the situation there is difficult and the salary not good." They said that in Nawsad, the Taliban is lenient compared to Kabul and Jalalabad. "Here there is singing, dancing, freedom," Wasea the nurse told us. The only complaint the Taliban has had in Nawsad, the doctor explained, is that their medical stores are not as successful since the clinic opened.

The women in all the villages use this clinic for basic health care, though it is far away for some families. They are charged a fee of Afs.2500[30] when they first register and Afs.500[31] for consecutive visits. The doctor also makes house calls. More serious cases are treated in Lashkargah, Grishk, Kandahar, or Pakistan. But not everyone is convinced by the health care available in Nawsad. Bibi Ayesha (40, G 1) tartly stated that what they need in Nawsad is "a proper hospital with a real doctor."

Bibigula (28, DM 10) suspects that the reason she has no living child after four pregnancies and deliveries is due to a "lack of proper health services."

Due to the female staff at the hospital, travel out of Nawsad for basic health care is no longer necessary. The presence of female medical staff appeases the Taliban as far as restrictions for women being treated by female doctors goes. However, inside the clinic women go to see, and are treated by, the male doctor as well as the female nurse. The women say that they don't believe that a woman could be a qualified doctor. They also say that the male doctor is *mahram* for them. According to the doctor they receive between 10-20 female patients daily. Those living far away or in the bazaar arrive in a *burqa*. The local women nearby use a *chadar*. Women have no restrictions to access to health care, but because of the distance to the clinic from some of the villages, women like Jawahera (60, J 3), "just wait, then if it is serious, I go to the doctor."

Refugee Villages

The refugee villages in Baluchistan have BHUs. Either Mercy Corps or the Project Directorate of Health of the Pakistani Government[32] manage the BHUs. The services provided by the BHUs include an open patient department (OPD), immunization, mother/child health (MCH), and training of volunteer male and female community health workers in preventative health care. Disabled men, women and children benefit from daily physical rehabilitation services at the BHU. This programme is community based. At least one family member of the patient is taught physiotherapy exercises. There is also a system for patient referrals from the field to hospitals in Quetta and an orthopedic workshop that provides devices to the disabled.

The immunization programme has been very successful. Men and women bring their children to the BHU for vaccinations. On national immunization days, the BHUs are congested with both men and women bringing their own and the neighbours' children, often loaded into wheelbarrows. Polio can be considered eradicated. No new cases have emerged in the refugee villages over the past two years. Any new cases registered have all been recent arrivals from Afghanistan.

The refugee community has been active in maintaining the health services at a high standard. They contribute financially for the services by paying for medicines and consultations with the doctor. The community has been active in solving problems related to health provision. In the refugee village Surkhab, the Taliban visited BHUs to check that only female doctors treated women. At one stage they put pressure on the BHUs to be closed down but were stopped by the community. As the Taliban had no intentions or capacity to provide alternative health care for the village, the community refused to let the Taliban interfere with existing service provisions.

Reproductive Health

Women deliver their first child very young. Most first time mothers are teenagers. The average marriage age among the women is 15.5 years (see Appendix III).

Women refer to having children when they themselves are still children. They speak of how difficult it was as a child to take the responsibility for taking care of children and a husband.

"People like us in the village have no childhood because early marriage spoils life," Shabnam (42, DM 6).

"I had a nice time when I was a child. I'm just kidding. They forced me to marry when I was nine years old. Nice childhood full of enjoyment," Badra (41, L 2) adds sarcastically.

"We were poor, that's why they married me when I was ten. As a child, I was the wife of a man and had children," Shahperai (50, HAZ 58).

"I had a good mother and father, they did not marry me when I was a child . . . I was 20," Hazrata (36, HAZ 43).

"I did not have any childhood. When I was ten I married. So I was not a child any more. I was someone's wife," Zar Malik (60, TA 8).

"I was lucky that I got married when I was 18," Khora (53, DZ 3).

"I had a nice childhood; no war, no responsibility. And as a child I married [at 12]. This is a very bad tradition to marry at such a young age," Sharaba (42, G 3).

"I was born in Kajaki and brought up there. Since 15 years we live in Hazarjuft. I was very happy when I was a child. I was thinking to enjoy it but I got married . . . when I was 13 . . . when you are a child someone has to take care of you, but as a child you have to take care of another; a husband and a child. My children lost their father when they were too young . . . so the war also joined their life," Gulgulab (40, HAZ 31).

Women are starting to change lives for their daughters by not marrying them so young and encouraging family planning.

"My children, girls, have not married in their childhood," Rasto (37, L 4).

"I didn't have a good childhood. When I was ten years old my parents married me by force. A lot of change. Now I wish that I should not do what my parents did," Niekbakhta (50, G 2).

"I did not have a childhood. I was a married woman. I should have been playing with children but I could not. At least people are aware that their children should not marry when they are children, they should enjoy their childhood ... I was seven years old [when I married]," Bibi Tahira (55, HAZ 33).

"I enjoyed my childhood, but 15 years old is not the age for marriage," Bibigula (45, HAZ 34).

"I enjoyed my childhood ... [I was] married when I was seven ... in my in-laws house – awful. I know at least now that I should not arrange marriage for my children in the ages between seven and 12," Shahwazira (37, TA 3).

"Less children is good. We can enjoy life," Shafiqa (20, DM 7).

"My life is fine but I have too many children [ten]," Bulbula (41, LO 1).

Most women have had home deliveries. Previously in Helmand, there were no community health workers trained in safe motherhood to assist births as there are in the refugee villages. Now the Hazarjuft hospital, staff carries out male and female community health worker training.

"[In Pakistan] we had a trained dai[33] but here not. [In the refugee village] they could get re-supplies from the BHU. Here, it is very difficult for a home delivery to be safe and clean," Azmat (30, HAZ 22).

"It is different here. We don't have home visits from the hospital and no traditional birth attendants," says Kulsooma (30, HAZ 42) who in her ten years of marriage has not had a single live birth.

Women who have complications during birth are occasionally taken to Lashkargah. In Kobra's case (17, DB 9), she travelled all the way to Quetta. "I gave [birth] by caesarean section in Lashkargah then the wound got infected. I went to Quetta – Zoya Hospital. After four months my son died." At that time she was five months pregnant again.

Complicated births can be dealt with in the Hazarjuft hospital. "It is different in Afghanistan and refugee villages. Here, we have a doctor for deliveries in the village, but in the refugee village just a qualified nurse," Nadia (40, HAZ 35).

Women are aware of birth control and diseases such as AIDS, less aware of other sexually transmitted diseases (STDs). This is largely due to BBC radio and awareness that women who have repatriated from refugee villages are spreading. The incidence of STDs and AIDS is not clearly known. Despite awareness, women are often unable to act due to the unavailability of contraception or pressure from their husbands or older family members. In 1998, one 26-year-old woman in Lashkargah told of her efforts to not get pregnant after having had two children and after her husband moved out to begin a relationship with another woman. Her denying intercourse only resulted in beating. She was expecting her third child and lived alone with her in-laws.

The option of contraception is relatively new in village communities in Afghanistan, as Bora (30, G 4) explains, "[I was married] at 15 and gave birth very soon after. At that time we even did not know about contraceptives but my daughter-in-law and daughter are spacing their children by using pills and injections."

Anargula (25, G 8), mother of three, is pleased with contraceptives, "My life now is OK. I do child spacing and enjoy life."

According to the medical staff at the Absina clinic in Nawsad, women are coming for contraceptives, mostly for the pill. These women either do not want to have any more children, or use contraceptives for spacing. Other contraceptives are available, but it is not known to what extent they are used – at least for the purpose of contraception. In Deh Baloch, a young girl was playing with a "condom balloon" along one of the village paths.

Khora (38, J 1), a mother of ten, complains that her husband does not bring her contraceptives. Mahgul (30, J 2) has 11 children and says she is keen to stop having a child almost every year. Khor Bibi (20, HAZ 26) requests training in child spacing and the use of contraceptives. She has had six children in seven years. Bulbula (41, LO 1) is one of a number of women who feels her life would be easier if she had less than her ten children. She wants to encourage others not to have as many, "I want that others, young ladies, should not have more children."

In refugee villages, Mercy Corps has been carrying out a reproductive health programme since 1997. Reproductive health awareness is given to the community through various activities of the community development programme. Community health worker training is carried out. Safe motherhood, family planning, STDs/AIDS, and sexual violence prevention are central subjects in their curriculum. Male and female health management committees have been formed partly for the purpose of discussing reproductive health issues. Mercy Corps' female staff and community volunteers spend much of their time discussing these issues also with the men: committee and community members, elders, religious leaders, even the Taliban.

Contraceptives are distributed in BHUs. In the refugee villages, women prefer the pill and injections. In 2000, the prevalence rate of oral and injectable contraceptives was 4% among women between the ages of 15 and 45. Though the prevalence rate is low there has been a 780% increase in the use of oral and injectable contraceptives in the refugee villages since 1998. Intra-uterine devises (IUDs) are unpopular and can be problematic due to possible infections. There is some interest in tubal ligations however, men are very reluctant to get sterilised. Over the past year, there has been an increase in the use of contraception by younger women who have only a few children (one to three). Previously, most users had six to eight children before they began to use contraception. There has also been an increase in the use of contraceptives for spacing and STDs. One wife of a migrant labourer in Surkhab, who had a STD, complained about the difficulties of convincing her husband's second wife to also have protected sex.

Some women who drop out of BHU records keep using contraceptives. They find it more private to go and purchase the pill from the local medical stores in the bazaar instead of coming to the BHU.

Though men are receiving awareness, they are more timid to request for services. Women have done this on their behalf. They requested that *drishi*[34] be available on the desk of the female medical officer. This would enable women to come and get condoms, as "our men will be too shy," they explain. In October 1999, female community members brought to our attention a new problem: they asked for advice on what to do when their men complain that they do not get as much pleasure when using the condom.

Love affairs, rape, homosexuality, and incest occur within these communities. Women say it is not common but it does happen. Cases of rape that result in pregnancy are often the only ones that come to light. Particularly if the woman is unmarried, the situation is very complicated. According to Pushtoon culture, adulterers should be killed. In these cases it is usually the woman's life that is most at risk. Loss of female virtue means loss of face and family honour, *izzat*. In addition, it is difficult to arrange a marriage for an unmarried woman who is no longer a virgin. As some families survive off the brideprice of their daughters, *wulwar*, this means a significant loss in family income. But it is not only young unmarried women who are at risk. One 40-year-old woman told me that her 20-year-old nephew had raped her.

Women attempt to handle these situations within women's networks, without letting men know and without getting men involved. They say that if the men find out, they will at least beat the girl and almost certainly kill the man or force him to marry her. The man who violates is often a close relative – usually a cousin or an uncle. Gulanar (40) a refugee woman says, "It is necessary and our duty to give awareness to our sons. They are the ones who attack. We should pay attention to who they have contact with."

If a young woman who has become pregnant as a result of rape or a love affair is able to confide in an older woman, arrangements will be made for an abortion. "This is to save *izzat*," women explain. Upon marriage women use their imagination to explain why the bride is no longer a virgin. In one case, an older female relative that an unmarried pregnant girl had confided in said that she would explain to the girl's future mother-in-law that the girl had had an operation for a tumour that the doctor had to remove through the vagina. She laughed and said that it would be easy to explain because these people are uneducated. "They will believe anything." Among wealthier women, abortion is also used as a form of birth control. The medical staff in Nawsad reported a few requests for abortions but had not carried out any or investigated the exact circumstances of the women requesting them.

Another option is for the girl to "disappear" somewhere until she has given birth and given the baby away. There is much demand for babies among women who are childless, within the community as well as outside it. Adoption is uncomplicated. However, sending the girl away from home during her confinement is usually a difficult and rare option, particularly in displaced communities.

The third option is "hide and deliver." In one case the mother of a rape victim took an older experienced *dai* in her confidence. The pregnant girl kept her growing stomach hidden under folds of her *kamiz,* wore a large *chadar* and didn't socialise outside her compound for the period of her pregnancy. When the time of the birth came, the *dai* delivered the child in her home, took the baby and gave it to the girl's married sister who had had a miscarriage but been instructed not to tell anyone about it. The *dai* then spread word around the village that the sister had given birth that morning. She had delivered a healthy child. "No one questioned me and no one else knows what really happened to this day," the *dai* told me.

Exceptions to rules regarding sex before the wedding ceremony exist among the Pushtoon. *Pshah khalas* is an old tradition still practised by some Pushtoon families. The literal meaning of *pshah khalas* is that a man has "a leg free" to enter the house of his bride before the marriage ceremony. The bride's mother can give an engaged couple permission to see each other, even have sexual contact in the bride's father's house before marriage. An amount of the brideprice has to be paid before this is allowed. The promise of sex before the actual marriage ceremony is occasionally used as an incentive for quick payment of the brideprice. Women are not sure of the exact origin of this practice, but they say that one reason for practising *pshah khalas* is to help a young bride become accustomed to her new life as a wife gradually, in the safety of her own family home. Because the official marriage contract, *nikah*, is signed at the engagement and marriage predominantly arranged between relatives, or families living close by, any risks involved in the practice of *pshah khalas* are securely within the control of the joint family and community.

The engagement can last anywhere from three months to over a year. During the period of *pshah khalas*, while living in her father's house, a woman is allowed to refuse sex, something women say they cannot do when they are married. If a woman gets pregnant during the engagement, the wedding is arranged immediately.

Traditional Healing and Tension Release

"Tension is with every lady. No way to get out," Sherina (45, DM 3).

In 1998, all women interviewed complained that there is a lack of good quality medicines in Afghanistan. In 1999, it was limited to complaints that the hospital and BHUs did not stock everything available in the open market. Women increasingly use pharmaceuticals as well as traditional methods for healing and releasing stress and tension.

Minor ailments are usually cured by a visit to the Mullah or by taking medicines bought at a medical store in the bazaar. Some women have learned how to give injections. Older women also advise younger women where they can, prescribe home remedies, or do *dums*. A *dum* is saying words of the Quran and blowing at a person. Home remedies include drinking the blood of a rabbit for breathing problems such as asthma. Sand, earth or mud from the grave of a *bazurk* or *pir*, a holy or very religious person, can be used in various ways. It can be put into amulets or smeared on the skin to cure or ward off illness. Young children are often wrapped in the skin of a goat to rid the child of a fever.

The Mullah will offer prayers and give a *taweez*, amulet, or do a *dum*. One child in Loralai had a whole row of *taweez* around the neck. Verses of the Quran were folded into triangular shapes and sewn inside colourful pieces of cloth. These were to cure and ward off polio and general illness. A garlic clove was to ward off Hepatitis; Ziarat salt for curing any type of disease.

It became clear during our stay in Nawsad that women there are particularly prone to the abuse of pharmaceuticals. For example, Hussungula (44, DB 8) takes 5mg of Diazepam (Valium) daily for tension and Pakiza (45, DB 3) regularly takes 15mg of Tranxen (Dipotassium Clorazepate) despite her son's warnings that she will become addicted.

The use of strong prescription medicines for minor ailments is alarming. Shopkeepers of medical stores, rarely qualified pharmacists, recommend a range of medicines, often the most expensive, to make their business profitable and to ensure cure. As people are unable to choose the type of medicine they need, and because they can afford it, they end up buying every item recommended.

During our stay with a family in Nawsad, their 14-year-old daughter approached us. She asked if we could help her with an injection for a minor cold. She told us she had learned to give injections by watching her father inject cows, but she was having difficulty injecting her own arm. On closer inspection the vial contained strong antibiotics. Having given her an Actifed (for congestion and cold) instead, her aunt sat down next to us for tea and began swallowing the remaining pills of Actifed, for a pain in her thigh!

Pharmaceuticals have gained a new status in this area of Afghanistan. This is illustrated by the fact that in all of the households visited in Nawsad, medicines are hung on the wall in plastic bags on display like all the other wealth of the household: crockery, cutlery, photographs, pieces of embroidery, carpets, cushions, mattresses, and even shoes in one household.

A number of the older women use *nuswar*,[35] and a wide range of "tonics" to release tension. Nine women of those interviewed in

Afghanistan had used *nuswar*. Two of these women had stopped using it. Shakar (60, G 10) had stopped after she heard on BBC radio that *nuswar* is one cause of cancer. Ram Bibi (59, DM 2) complained how difficult it is to stop using once you have started. She explained that when she lost her husband "other women told me *nuswar* is a good thing to get you away from tension." Badro (60, TA 1) explained that she uses *nuswar* because "when a person is a widow, she has a lot of tension."

One woman (Bibigula 28, DM 10) said she smokes the *hookah*, a water pipe for tobacco. Spozmai (30, DB 6) stopped smoking the *hookah* when she married three years ago. Some of the young unmarried girls smoke cigarettes in secret. In the household of our hosts in Nawsad, after the parents had gone to bed, the adolescent girls sat together outside in the courtyard gossiping and smoking cigarettes.

Women traditionally use poppy water (opium extracted from poppy pods by boiling) to tranquilize babies or young children who are cranky or cannot sleep. With the awareness in health care and anti-poppy propaganda, another problem has emerged. Women are now giving children antibiotic and codeine-based syrups, which make children immune to the effects of these medicines when they are prescribed for illness. Some chew opium, but women said that generally they do not use hard drugs. Sabira (43, DB 1) explains that in Nawsad she goes "sometimes to see the doctor. He gives some tonic. Since the Taliban are here nobody uses drugs. Before a few people were using hashish."[36]

The majority of women still say that the best way to rid oneself of agitation and tension is to sleep, become aggressive, visit neighbours, or beat the children.

The Value of Two Opium Eaters is One Penny

Drug addiction is not acceptable within Afghan community, as a Pushtoon proverb indicates, "A son who takes hashish is no son, and the value of two opium eaters is one penny."

Addiction to drugs is most clearly seen in the refugee villages. Still, more often than not, addiction afflicts young men who became addicted to opium, heroin, or smoking *charas* or *hashish*[37] while doing labour in the Sindh or Punjab provinces of Pakistan or Iran. This is usually the first time they have traveled far away from their village and are without any kind of support from their community and family.

Cases of female addiction have come to light. Wives and children of male addicts are often secondary users, as they inhale the drugs that the male addict smokes in the household.

In Pir Alizai, which is located on the Chaman road, a centre for drug trafficking, the problem is the most acute. Tribal warfare and Pakistani traffickers coming to collect their loot add to the instability of the village. As an indication of the breadth of the problem, five out of eleven women of a recently trained group of volunteer community health workers had an immediate family member, either husband, son or son-in-law who was addicted. The drugs most commonly used are opium, heroin, *charas*, and *hashish*. Of these five, one woman's husband became addicted six years ago and has recently disappeared. Another's husband has been using drugs for 20 years. He became addicted in Mazar. The third woman's son became addicted in the refugee village and left for Afghanistan with the Taliban. The fourth woman's son became addicted while doing labour in Karachi. The husband and son-in-law of the fifth woman use any drugs they can get their hands on.

Drug abuse in the other refugee villages is much more controlled by the social pressures and laws in the village. In Chagai, another hotbed for trafficking, smuggling and processing drugs, the number of addicts is not as great as in Pir Alizai. The elders and health committee members carry out drug harm reduction and rehabilitation. I talked to two former heroin and opium addicts, both young men in their 20s. The committee had persuaded one of them to stop using drugs completely. The other young man laughed as he told me that yes, he no longer used heroin or opium, thanks to the committee, but what they didn't know was that he now smoked *charas* instead. The elders, if unable to stop a community member from using drugs, hand the addict over to the Taliban who lock him up until he has been detoxicated. They claim a very high success rate as long as the former addict remains in the village. Another elder in Surkhab forced an addict to leave the village as he was setting a bad example to the younger members of the community.

Women also participate in the rehabilitation of drug addicts in very practical ways. Due to the joint efforts of two women in Surkhab, three men had stopped heroin smuggling and using drugs. The incentive provided by these women was alternative employment. One of the heroin smugglers is now buying wool for women to spin. Fifty women are now involved in this business. Dozens of women are attempting to persuade their husbands and sons to stop using *nuswar* and to stop smoking cigarettes. One woman persistently filled her husband's round metal *nuswar* container with dried grass until he gave in.

It is evident that the internal cohesiveness of the community has a direct effect on the use of drugs. In villages that are populated predominately by one ethnic group or one tribe, the problem of drugs is non-existent. Also, populations that have come from areas within Afghanistan that are traditionally non-poppy producing areas face fewer problems of addiction. A good example of this is Saranan, where the population is predominantly one tribe from Saripul, in northern Afghanistan.

---

[26] This work has been funded by the US Bureau for Population, Refugees and Migration.

[27] $0.15 US Dollars (USD).

[28] $0.16 USD.

[29] $3.26 USD.

[30] $0.04 USD.

[31] $0.008 USD.

[32] The health programmes of both agencies in the refugee villages is funded by the United Nations High Commissioner for Refugees (UNHCR).

[33] Traditional birth attendant.

[34] *Drishi* is the Pushto word that women use for condom. It means a "suit for men."

[35] Chewing tobacco.

[36] Cannabis.

[37] Both *charas* and *hashish* are cannabis.

— 7 —

Education

In the rural areas of Helmand, education has never been a priority. Selma Bibi, a refugee in Surkhab, explained that in rural areas of Afghanistan, the priority has always been, "skills first, then school." How to work on the land, in the household, or within the family trade is survival. Prior to the war, education and health care facilities were concentrated in the big cities, such as Kabul, Ghazni, Mazar, Herat, and Kandahar. Women associate education with working outside the home.

It is only since the Taliban came into power, when the few schools that did exist were closed down, that these rural women have become more aware and concerned about education.

"I think women in Kabul wanted to be educated, they need education for earning money too. We had lands and we were unaware of the value of education," Belqisa (30, SUR 4).

"I'm allowed to go everywhere but I can't work because I am not educated and not young," Kheshmesh (70, DA 2).

"I live for my child. I hope he can get education and work in an office, not like his father working on other's land," Shafiqa (20, DM 7).

During the war, access to education in many areas was virtually impossible due to fighting and the mobility of the displaced population. Women stress the importance of education and express interest in it, but say that they need and want access to basic needs first. After that, it is time to think of education. As Bibi Ayesha (26, SAR 2) says, "When there is peace we will think of education."

The most motivated women are those whose children have received education in refugee villages or who themselves are originally from outside Nawsad or Garamser. Durkhanai and Bibi Borjana have both returned to Hazarjuft after 15 years in Pakistan.

"My life as a child was OK. I had everything but my only wish was education. That I never reached. Dreams come to my mind that my children will be educated," Durkhanai (48, DA 3).

"My children have a peaceful life and I want them to be educated, but I think it is just a dream," Bibi Borjana (30, DA 4).

Qandi (45, DM 4) was born and brought up in Kandahar. She was married to a man in Nawsad when she was ten and never went to school herself, but all her brothers graduated from high school. She made sure that her own children received education. Her children are high school graduates and one studies medicine at University.

Education is equated with the possibility for children to lead a better life and to gain greater awareness of life. Refugee life and BBC radio have had an important role in teaching about the importance of education.

"My childhood was very funny. We did not know about anything, now look at children. They know everything. When I got married I did not know what it meant. I thought that I'm a guest there. After one week I wanted to go back home. Now even a child of five knows," Rangina (95, HAZ 7).

The value of education is also tied to a perception that it allows the possibility for easier jobs with better pay. Refugees in particular have seen the educated members of their communities being hired by aid and development agencies in the refugee villages or employed in offices in Quetta. Getting respect through education is also a factor.

Women themselves might not express a desire to learn how to read and write, but stress that it would be good if their children were given the opportunity. Some women lament how different their lives could have been had they had an opportunity to go to school.

"You know my sons are Talibs and I am in favour of education for both sexes. But look, I am uneducated, I have not even asked my sons why they don't allow education for women," Bibigula (55, HAZ 4).

Lamenting, Bibigula shook her head, saying she would ask as soon as she saw her sons again. Even women who have lived their whole life in their village of origin and who do not have any family members who have been formally educated, express interest, "I want to send my children to school but there are no facilities," Mahgul (30, J 2).

Older women want to leave education to their younger family members. They say they no longer have the energy, "I have time but I'm too old. I won't participate [in any new training] because I am too old," Sahiba (60, L I).

Many also feel that illiteracy impairs the ability to learn new things. "It is important to learn, but I am uneducated, can I learn?" Shahwariza (37, TA 3).

Northern Helmand

In Nawsad, only one of the women had had any form of formal education or adult literacy. Gulmakai (38, J 8) was brought up in Mazar-i-Sharif and went to primary school before her marriage when she was ten years old. The majority of men in Nawsad are also illiterate. Generally, the highest level of education that the husband of an interviewee had was secondary school. Only the husband of Nasrin (30, J 5) had studied for 16 years in Kabul and Kandahar, but she didn't know exactly what he had studied, and the husband of Gulzada (41, DB 5) is a Lashkargah trained nurse.

There are *madrassas*, religious schools, for boys in Nawsad but they do not seem to be very popular. Shireen in Dehmian said, "I made the mistake of sending him [son] to *madrassa*. He is out of my control. If there had been a school, I would have sent him there." Mahgul told us that her husband insisted all their children, three girls and four boys attend *madrassa*.

More often, children are needed at home to help with chores. "I had a very nice childhood, no responsibility. Happy. No war. A lot has changed . . . now a sense of responsibility. Even a child of seven has to take care of his or her family. Poverty. Awareness. We had a chance for education and did not want it. Our children want it but . . . ," Feroza (42, TA 9).

Young children do not work regularly in the fields, though they do act as messengers and bring food from home for the labourers. Children pick fruit and almonds from trees in the orchards and help women with many tasks in the house and compound. Boys work with women in the compound and orchards until they are nine or ten years old. Watching the daily routines of the family with which we lived, every child had his/her own responsibility. Young boys killed the chickens and took food to the male side of the house if there were guests. Girls brought water, swept the floors, carried wood, and took care of their younger siblings. Young boys and girls bring alfalfa from the fields for livestock and they milk goats and cows. Adolescent girls cook, lay bedding down at dusk, wrap it away at dawn and wash clothes. Girls do embroidery for cushion covers, wall hangings and clothes. As we were going to bed on platforms made of branches outside in the courtyard, a six-year-old girl proudly showed off the cushion cover she had embroidered for herself.

Children learn the skills necessary for life by watching their elder siblings and adults. Few adults have much time for teaching. Children themselves are interested in education. "They are not blind, we were blind," Khaldara (62, HAZ 28).

Two mothers told us the following:

"[The children] want to be educated but we don't have access to that. No schools. We did not give value to education," Khora (38, J 1).

"There aren't many changes in life [as my children have grown older], but the children are interested in education," Gulmakai (38, J 8).

Southern Helmand

All the women interviewed in Nad-i-Ali were illiterate. In Lashkargah three of the women had between six to ten years of formal education. In Grishk, one woman had finished school in the eighth grade, three women were college graduates. Two were qualified as teachers. One woman, the wife of a Talib, had been to *madrassa*, taught by her husband. She stated that she no longer believed in the benefits of female education.

In Hazarjuft, three women out of 58 interviewed had primary or secondary school education, the rest were illiterate, never having attended formal or informal education. One of these educated women, Pargula (18, HAZ 25), was brought up in Kabul. Her husband and brothers were also educated. Her own son is still too young to attend school. Saliqa (19, HAZ 27) was brought up in Lashkargah where she completed fifth grade, and then the school was shut down. She is now married to an educated man in Hazarjuft and is six months pregnant. Fifteen women had either a brother, husband or father-in-law who had received at least primary school education. The highest level of education among these men was the brother of Roshana (35, HAZ 50) who was a University graduate. Ten of the husbands were technical college graduates.

The children of 12 women had received schooling. Six of these families repatriated from Pakistan. Two families educated their daughters also. The daughters and sons of Mahjan (40, HAZ 44) went to school in Laghman, before they moved to Hazarjuft. Now her sons go to *madrassa*. She is concerned that at least her sons should receive the education available. Qandigul's (36, HAZ 32) daughters attended home-based schools before the family moved to Hazarjuft, where there are no equivalent schools available. Another woman's daughters had only attended school in Pakistan. Five women had sons in *madrassas*. Two women had brothers who had gone to a *madrassa*, one's husband had been through *madrassa* education. *Madrassa* is not an option for everyone. Azmat (30, HAZ 22) complained that, "We have peace but no school for the boys."

Returnees from Pakistan complain that their children's education came to a halt when they returned to Afghanistan either because there were no schools to attend, or because children had to enter the labour force. "We don't have schools here. In the refugee village we asked for a school, but when they decided to make a school we came back to Afghanistan," Sharifa, (30, HAZ 6).

In Grishk, two families had sent their children to school but they had not completed their education due to the war. One family's children had gone to *madrassa*, one had completed college, and one completed secondary school. Two families educated only their sons: one through formal education the other in the *madrassa*. Other women said they had not been able to send their offspring to school because of poverty and the security situation. Spozhmai (40, GRI 5), a qualified teacher, is secretly homeschooling her children four hours a day.

In Lashkargah, the children of four women had attended school but the girls had stopped when the Taliban forbade co-education. Boys are still attending school. One woman sent her daughters to the *madrassa* when the Taliban closed the school. Another woman's son had completed college, but his siblings had to work after primary school to supplement family income. Another young man completed eighth grade and then had to look for work when his mother was widowed.

Refugee Villages

All the women interviewed in 1998 in Pir Alizai, Saranan, and Surkhab were illiterate, but some of the women are now attending non-formal education centres. There is much demand among refugee women for literacy as well as learning more about health care, kitchen gardens and rearing small animals.

The refugee villages have primary education schools for boys and girls, home-based girl schools, and non-formal education centres. These are run by Save the Children (US). In the refugee villages, some women send their daughters to school due to incentives, such as edible oil that is given to each girl who attends school. Some families are known to have left a daughter in the refugee village with relatives, when the family repatriates, in order to get the regular supply of edible oil. As Bibi Hawa (49, SAR 6) explains, "Primary education is allowed for girls. But you have to know, here [in Pakistan], women don't have restrictions and women know the value of education, but our men don't allow us. Just because of some incentives, our daughters go to school."

In Surkhab refugee village, the Taliban threatened to cut the hands off of any parents who send daughters older than ten to school. This caused outrage, particularly among women. The issue was resolved within the community. Salma Bibi (58, SUR 3), a community health committee member, feels that it is not only the Taliban that are to blame, "Of course, girls and women are not allowed to get education, but we can't blame only the Taliban. Before the people in villages did not want to get education because of culture or tradition. I don't know. But now we know that everyone has to get education. Education is necessary for survival."

Women in the refugee villages feel that for training or education for women to take place in Afghanistan, it would have to be sanctioned by the Taliban and their husbands. Women inside Afghanistan feel that training and education would not be a problem as long as it was carried out by a female and held in someone's home compound.

Constraints

The Taliban have closed down the few schools that did exist in the rural areas. However, women are keen to point out that they themselves are in part to blame for the lack of formal education in their communities, through lack of interest. Women explain that during the pre-war era, culture, tradition and childhood influence prohibited interest in, and understanding of, the value of health care and education. "Before the war, education was free and allowed but because of culture, we did not want to study," Totia (30, SUR 1).

"[Before the war, there was] access but we did not want to be educated. We were thinking that education is not good for women, but now we know it is necessary. [During the war,] there was no access to education in the villages. [Now,] there is no access to education, but at this stage we want our basic needs," Monawar (48, SUR 5).

"Many changes during the war and life gets worse, violence, killing each other, but then the Taliban came. Education is restricted but in villages we did not have education before for females. It does not make a difference for us," Mahgula (45, HAZ 2).

Women also remind themselves of the community's role in restrictions to education.

"The restrictions are not only the Taliban's. Who makes the government? Of course, society. Who is society? Of course, community. So our society does not prefer education for women, only people in cities want female education. Even if we shout that we want to get education, we can't get it. We should realise we are living in a male-dominated society," Negora (32, SAR 13).

For many, family restrictions are too great an obstacle to overcome.

"We didn't have a good childhood. The only [good] thing was peace. We could not get education or have a good life. We were from a poor family, my husband too. As time went by, I knew that education is a must for both sexes, but my father-in-law did not allow us to send our daughters to school. When he died, the situation had changed. . . . We can see positive and negative changes. As people living in the village, we did not have value as human beings but now we are aware of everything. We did not know about TV, but now our young children know about it . . . now we have different models of cars on the roads. But the negative is that our young generation can't get education. This is now desired. First we wanted peace. Now we have it. Before the Taliban, women and girls were under sexual violence. We were powerless. Their [Mujahedin] language was the gun and killing people," Khadija (42, HAZ 1).

In the refugee villages, the need for income effects children's education. Some children are sent for a few months of the year to

Karachi as garbage collectors. Girls continue to be engaged for marriage at a young age and are often taken out of school once engaged. Girls particularly are involved in income-generating activities such as spinning wool.

Concern is expressed by women that despite interest in learning new skills or becoming literate, they do not have time to participate in such activities.

"I have six children to take care of, I do others' house work and take care of in-laws. This is a lot of work for me. I don't have time but look, my in-laws, they will participate. They are interested. Everywhere they are looking for some training. When you entered our house, they were thinking you are talking of such training and they told me 'please write our name too,' " Shafiqa (35, Las 4).

There are women who do not believe in female education because they feel that as women, they have the right not to have to worry about livelihood and security.

"We women and girls, we are not allowed [to go to school]. It is not allowed in our society. Powerless women. But on the other hand, it is good that we are at home and the husband, father and brothers earn money. Why should we waste our energy? Look at yourself [Dr. Yasmin] how you look tired and too far from your family. I think that even at this stage you don't have security. This is because of education," Basira (19, HAZ 16).

— 8 —

Women's Work and Divisions of Labour

Family as a Unit of Production

The concept of family among the Pushtoon differs from the western definition of family. It is relevant to understand these definitions as they help explain the position of women in relation to men at different times in their lives. In Pushtoon culture, over the course of one's life, a man and a woman may be considered a member of a number of different families. Being a member of one family unit depends on residence, marital status and labour.

There are two words for the English word "family" in Pushto and Dari. The first, *khanadan*, is used to refer to all those people who live in the same compound, within the same walls. These people may or may not be related by blood or marriage. The word *famil* or *koronai* (Pushto) is used to refer to all those who sit at the same table, *dasterkhan*.[38] In other words, those who share their resources and income with each other form one *famil*. In some cases, this includes what in the west is referred to as a nuclear family. However, more often than not *famil* includes a grandparent, aunts and uncles, or perhaps a cousin, as well as more than one wife if the man has married a few times. The defining factor for being a member of one *famil* is contributing money and labour to that unit and sharing meals.

Daughters cease to be *famil* when they are married and move to another household. Sons who do not live in their father's house are also no longer *famil*. If they return and contribute financially to their father's household, they will regain their status as family members. This explains to some extent why educating daughters is considered to be watering the neighbours garden. The benefit of education ultimately goes to another household. "Not good, no son, no life. Daughters [seven] go to other's houses," Roqia (43, HAZ 52).

The most important role of a woman is that of mother and wife. Her status improves as she marries and becomes a mother. There are many Pushto proverbs that glorify wives and motherhood. A few examples include: "Paradise is under the feet of a mother;" "The arms of a woman are the first *madrassa* (school) of a child;" and "The *rahmat farishta* (angel of blessing) does not put his foot in a home with no women."

The brideprice, *wulwar*, received by the girl's parents from the groom's family upon marriage is an important income for many Afghans, both in refugee villages and in rural Afghanistan. Many families survive on the income from their daughter's marriages. "[Life is] now not good – poverty. Living with the money of *wulwar* of daughters," Jawahir (45, HAZ 53).

The increased income from opium production has caused the brideprice to soar in many villages of rural Afghanistan. Wealthy landowners are requesting brideprices in the range of Rs.600,000-700,000.[39] Poorer families ask for Rs.100,000 – 200,000.[40] The daughter of one of our host families had just become engaged in Nawsad, for an agreed *wulwar* of Rs.400,000.[41] Most of this money returns to the groom's family in the form of the bride's dowry. The bride's family uses the *wulwar* to buy household items and clothes for the bride to take with her to her new home.

In the refugee villages, *wulwar* has become a way of supplementing a virtually non-existent household income. The rates in refugee villages tend to be between Rs.50,000 and Rs.300,000.[42] Men in refugee villages have requested Mercy Corps' community development workers for assistance in their attempts to convince women not to ask for such high brideprices. Women predominantly negotiate and arrange marriages within the community. Their brideprice demands often leave men in crippling debt.

Female Labour in Agricultural Production

Agriculture is the central form of income in southern Afghanistan. It provides income even to small land holders and the landless in the form of farm labour. The vast majority of the husbands, sons or brothers of the women interviewed do off-farm labour as well as cultivate their own lands (if they have land) and care for livestock. The drought that began in the spring of 2000 has caused a shortage of grazing, and as a result, the livestock has begun to die. This signifies a loss in family capital and income.

Rural men and women have interlinked roles in sustaining their livelihood; one cannot do without the other. The majority of women in southern Afghanistan do not work in the fields, but they have a role in the later stages of the production of crops, for instance, cleaning the seed. Men plant fruit trees, women pick and dry the fruit and men sell it. Despite not working on the land, women place a high value on land and the fact that lands lost during the war have been regained.

"Now it is OK. No war. Peace. And everybody is on his land. I can see my children with a smile on their lips," Feroza (42, TA 9).

Female labour and income-generating activities within Afghanistan are predominantly centred around the compound. Household compounds are divided into areas for the family or private space. For women, private space is called *zenana* in Dari or *shezina* in Pushto, and the male and guest side is known as *mardana* or *narina*. The contrast between the male and the female side of the rural compounds can be, but is not always, great. The men's side usually has a latrine. Women and children defecate around the living area, sometimes close to the household source of water, or in an orchard if it is attached to the house. The men's and guest side may have a garden or even buildings made from bricks, where the female side is more often made of mud. Male members of the family give women money for household expenses, food, and cloth for clothes. Few women are given money to improve the female side of the compound by building latrines or buying gas lamps to use for chores after dark.

Many men feel that women should earn their own money for "luxuries" that they desire. Women have become increasingly aware of available commodities and do not like to feel that they are missing out. "Before we didn't know what shampoo was, now we wash our hair with shampoo," Bibi Noor (50, DM).

In refugee villages, the compounds will usually have the family or female side, and one room for the guests, *saraitcha*. There are VIP latrines[43] in the majority of the compounds. In Loralai, where there are irrigation channels through some of the villages, such as Zar Karez, a platform with a hole in the middle has been built, like a bridge, over the running water as a latrine. This water is also used for the household.

Rural women lament the lack of electricity in their villages. Four women in Laki and the women in Nawsad mentioned how electricity would help them. They explained that electricity and a water source in their compound would give them more time for other activities. More work could be done in the night, not just before dusk.

"My life is not bad. The economic situation is better now but villagers don't have life like people in the city. . . . If I lived in the city, I'd have electricity and other facilities," Sharaba (42, G 3).

"Now [life] is not bad, but not good either. When I hear from others that there are women who have electricity, I am jealous and I think we are unlucky women who live here," Shamsa (40, G 7).

Women primarily tend kitchen gardens or rear animals within the compound (see Appendix IV). In some villages, particularly in Nawsad, the family orchards are attached to the household compound and surrounded by walls. Women and children pick the crop from trees. Agricultural produce is mainly used for household subsistence, but any excess is either sold or exchanged for other agricultural produce between neighbours or relatives.

In Grishk, women sell and exchange goods less than in the other research areas. Women say they could exchange goods, but they do not as they can afford to buy them from the bazaar. One woman added that it is not good for "city women" to deal with exchange. In Grishk, exchange of goods takes place most often when the household receives unexpected guests.

In Lashkargah, Nad-i-Ali and particularly Garamser, dairy products, vegetables and chickens are exchanged and sold within the community. Animals such as chickens, ducks, sheep, goats, cows, donkeys, and rabbits are reared. Two women in Garamser said that they used to rear rabbits but their men do not like rabbits because they dirty the compound.

In Afghanistan, women made the following distinctions between male and female labour and duties.

Men and boys older than ten years	Women, girls and boys younger than ten years
Pray	Put water to boil
Eat breakfast	Pray
Work in the fields/orchards/ shops/workshops	Make breakfast
Shop for the household	Clean the dishes, the house and children
Go to *Madrassa* and/or Mosque	Milk cattle
Sit and talk	Make lassi and yoghurt
Do repairs in the compound	Collect water
Teach children Islamiat	Clean crops/pick and dry fruit
Bring wood	Cook lunch
Eat	Wash dishes and clothes
Sleep	Sleep or visit with others
	Embroider, weave, spin
	Make tea
	Prepare dinner
	Clean up after dinner
	Make beds
	Sleep

In the refugee villages, the insufficient water supply has been a problem for growing vegetables, but the skills and interest in this exist. Refugees have no agricultural land in Pakistan. The male members of some families travel back to Afghanistan on a regular basis to cultivate their lands there. Refugee men work as labour in the orchards and fields of others. Despite this, a growing worry among the elder generation of refugees is the fact that they have brought up a generation with no attachment to land, a generation that has no skills to cultivate land. There is also concern that land distribution will be complicated upon repatriation as the older generation who tilled the land no longer exists to identify which land belonged to their family.

Refugee women would like to raise small animals in their courtyard but water again has limited the number of livestock. Most households have a goat or a sheep, some even have a cow. Chickens are reared but are considered difficult and dirty, and are thus less popular. In Afghanistan, these communities had agricultural lands and livestock.

Women and Poppy Production

The farmers in Nawsad began to grow poppy approximately thirty years ago for medicinal purposes. The government at the time placed strict restrictions on poppy cultivation. During the war, it became increasingly difficult to sustain livelihoods through traditional forms of subsistence, income-generation and labour. This coincided with the growth in demand for opium poppy and the lack of government control over poppy cultivation.

In addition to the formal interviews, informal discussions about poppy cultivation were held with 10-20 women each in Deh Baloch, Tangi Aulia and Dehmian, three villages in the poppy-growing district of Nawsad.

After 20 years of poppy cultivation for the drug trade, the mood is starting to change in Nawsad. Women express concern over the fact that it is un-Islamic, *haram*, to cultivate poppy and they are dissatisfied and fed up with the amount of extra work it creates for them personally.

Firoza in Tangi Aulia says, "I hate growing poppy. It is dirty. The income is dirty – *haram*. It is hard work. We are tired with the work and the labour is expensive and difficult to find."

During the lancing, *nish*, of poppy pods, specialised labour is hired by farmers to extract the opium. The women of the farmer's household are responsible for the wellbeing of all labourers on their family fields. In many cases this means 20-30 extra mouths to feed, three times a day. Women make the workers' beds at night and wash their clothes. Depending on the amount of land under poppy cultivation, lancing can take weeks to complete. Labour for lancing can be very expensive and very difficult to find, particularly in 1999, when the poppy in Nawsad and Garamser districts matured at the same time, instead of one area before the other. Labourers during a normal season are paid between Afs.50,000 –100,000[44] per day. During the last crop, they were able to raise their asking price considerably. This caused financial problems for some farmers.

A farmer in Tangi Aulia took a sizeable loan to pay for food, fertiliser, seed, and labour on his fields. He intended to repay the loan from poppy profits. He paid labourers to carry out lancing. He sold his crop but his profits only paid for half of the cost of labour. He was unable to pay his debt. As a result, he was forced to flee from the village and is in hiding – even his wife doesn't know where he is.

Poppy production has increased violence in the villages. Disputes over land have increased. This is not as much due to ownership issues, but to the economic value of what is grown on the land. A young widow, Torpaque, described her husband being shot dead three months previously by his cousin during a dispute over poppy cultivated land. Women explain that the reason for poppy cultivation is poverty. Shireen in Dehmian says, "Poppy is very *haram*, everybody knows it, but because of the situation, we grow it."

Other women state directly that they want to make as much money as possible. Most women however, see little of the benefits of the extra income in the family. Generally, women do not have access to this money, even though one woman (Durkhanai 48, DA 3) helps the men in her family count the money earned from poppy.

It is important to note that poppy cultivation in Nawsad has ceased to provide purely economic gain. Serious problems have begun to emerge within the community due to the cultivation of poppy. This is starting to make people nervous. Addiction among Afghan youth is beginning to emerge. Previously, addiction was seen as the problem of other people, not the producers of opium poppy. This has begun to change. People are afraid of divine punishment for carrying out something *haram*. The onset of drought may be seen as punishment. There are also fears that the new government may at some stage enforce strong laws against poppy cultivation. People are aware of the Taliban's methods of enforcing laws and know that no exceptions will be made if an edict is passed. There is silent acknowledgement that poppy cultivation in its present state will not go on forever. This was confirmed by the Taliban's ban on poppy cultivation at the end of 2000. During visits to Helmand province in the spring of 2001, no poppy could be seen.

Income-Generation

Women's contribution to the household economy may be important, but it comes only after her role and status as wife and mother. There is much interest among women in income-generating activities, even promises that an amount of poppy cultivation would be reduced if they were given the opportunity to earn extra income. The areas of particular interest were identified as chicken rearing, machine embroidery and sewing. Women would like to carry out these activities individually, as they feel group work might be difficult due to the restrictions placed on women by their husbands.

Women are involved in a number of income-generating activities, as can be seen in the table below.

Northern Helmand	Southern Helmand	Refugee Villages
Spinning wool	Spinning wool	Spinning wool
Embroidery	Embroidery	Embroidery
Making *chadars* and turbans for men	Making *chadars* and turbans for men	Making *tandoor* ovens
Making caps	Making caps	Making caps
Sewing clothes	Sewing clothes	Sewing clothes
	Knitting	Making weaning foods
	Weaving kilims (flat weave carpet)	Weaving kilims
	Buying and selling cosmetics, artificial jewelry, underwear	Buying and selling cosmetics, artificial jewelry, underwear
	Making bread	
	Domestic help	
	Leef, wash cloth	

The predominant income-generating activities of women are embroidery and making caps, as well as sewing and selling clothes. These items made by women are a symbol of personal esteem and are hung on the walls of houses or worn (by men and women) and admired by others. Some women act as "middle men" for women wanting to sell embroidery. In Afghanistan, only those in financial dire straits send their handiwork to be sold in the public bazaars. Refugee women also attempt to rely on sales of caps or embroidered *chadars,* dress front or sleeve pieces to supplement household income.

Women's income-generating activities usually form between 1-10% of the family or household income. There are a few cases of women whose income from embroidery formed 20% of the household income, but this is rare. The majority of household income is from agricultural crops or off-farm labour.

Women in Surkhab refugee village are unanimous about being allowed to work outside and inside the home or compound on income-generating activities. They state that due to poverty, they must also work outside the home, even if they were to return to Afghanistan. This is one reason they are not repatriating. What they explain as working outside their compound is predominantly selling or trading between households.

Women in refugee villages are involved in three major income-generating activities: embroidery, stitching clothes and making kilims (flat weave carpet). Women spin the wool, dye the wool and weave. The marketing and usually dyeing is left to male members of the family.

More recently, women have begun to make and sell *tandoors*, bread baking ovens. Women in Surkhab have begun a successful homemade chutney business. Women involved in food business are involved in teaching other women about weaning foods and hygiene.

Women on both sides of the border buy and sell cloth, artificial jewelry, underwear, soap, and Vaseline and sell it to other female community members. There are some old women that have small shops in their homes where they sell "women's items." At the same time, these women teach other women about female hygiene. Some of the items they sell are smuggled by male relations from Afghanistan, Iran or the Gulf, while other women travel to Quetta to purchase goods. One woman from Grishk travels to Pakistan to buy cosmetics and particularly hair removal cream, something she says men cannot buy for a woman. She has created a very successful business for herself.

Women work as household servants. Most of these women tend to be widows or very poor. Two women in Grishk bake bread for a wealthier household, while another washes clothes for others. One refugee woman had found a job for a widow and her two disabled sons as household servants in a wealthy Achekzai family in Quetta.

---

[38] *Dasterkhan* refers to the cloth or plastic sheet that food is placed on during a meal. It is spread on the floor of the home, either inside or outside in the courtyard. In this context, it is used to signify all those members of a family or household who eat together i.e., pool their resources.

[39] Between $11,700-$13,700 USD.

[40] Between $1,953-$3,900 USD.

[41] $7,813 USD.

[42] Between $970-$5,820 USD.

[43] A VIP latrine, a ventilated improved pit, is a mud hut with a deep pit below it. Inside, there is a hole in the ground and an air vent that reduces the smell.

[44] Between $0.81 - $1.60 USD.

— 9 —

Repatriation and Displacement

"We need respect as a woman and peace. We are tired of war, fighting. We want to go to our native land," Qadermanda (45, SAR 8).

The desire to return to Afghanistan is strong among refugees. However, uncertainty of sustaining a livelihood "at home" keeps Afghans in Pakistan. The most frequent reasons stated by women for not repatriating are: the expenses involved in moving and re-establishing a home, lack of employment, land, health care and education, difficulties for women to work outside the home, and the fact that everything in Afghanistan is expensive.

The lack of central government and the uncertain security situation are also brought up, particularly by women in Saranan, who are from the north where there is continued fighting. Recently, the drought has started to have an impact on repatriation.

In Pir Alizai, some of the people who repatriated have returned to Pakistan over the last year. They were unable to find work in Afghanistan. Family properties in Afghanistan were devastated and without work, people were unable to acquire the resources to rehabilitate their property and cultivate their lands.

A particular concern for women is the lack of health care facilities in Afghanistan. They say that at least in the refugee villages they can have a clean delivery with the help of a trained community health worker and have access to transportation in the case of an emergency. In their villages in Afghanistan, they have to rely on the services of the village *dai*, a traditional birth attendant.

A cause for great concern for families on both sides of the border is the Taliban's recruitment of men and adolescent boys for fighting. "Life is not bad but the big problem is our males being taken to war by Taliban," Azmat (30, HAZ 22). This is currently a significant reason for remaining in Pakistan. Families are reluctant to risk losing more family members to fighting. Too many sons, brothers and husbands have been lost to the war. In the south, the Taliban have been kidnapping adolescents, pressuring families to send their sons to fight, and forcing some to give up their land if they are unwilling to do so. One Hazara family in Hazarajat has sent their adolescent boys to live with relatives in Pakistan to be educated and to avoid possible conscription by the Taliban. The older men remained to till the land.

Of the formal interviews in 1999, four women said they have sons who are Taliban. One of these was from Nawsad, the rest from Garamser.

"I have sons and they are Talibs, so I am worried about them," Bibigula (55, HAZ 30).

"My life, it is OK now; near death's door. Surviving. One son was killed in the war, two of them are with Talibs and others are working in the field and shop . . . radio making shop," Kashmira (60, HAZ 19).

"My sons do off-farm labour, two of them. One is taken by Talibs," Kheshmesh (70, DA 2).

Two mothers in Hazarjuft told the following:

"My sons graduated from secondary school. They left it because of work or to attend the army for two years, then they came back to the village to hide themselves from the government," Khadija (42, HAZ 1).

"We don't like fighting and the Taliban take our young boys for fighting. This is a big problem," Sharifa (30, HAZ 6).

One young boy managed a narrow escape from a truck taking youths to the north in a busy market place, only because he knew the driver.

Of the 128 women formally interviewed in 1999, 31 had repatriated from Pakistan. Of these, two were in Laki and 29 from different villages in Garamser district. The exodus from the area was 16-

20 years ago. The refugees first began to return to this area seven or eight years ago, but most repatriation has occurred over the last three or four years. The fact that this coincides with the Taliban takeover is no coincidence. Under the Taliban, Helmand has been the most peaceful since before the war. There is acknowledgement, however, that the present peace in southern Afghanistan may not last.

Women that have repatriated seem generally mentally happier, more open and content compared to the women in refugee villages. In their own villages, they have more physical space, the surroundings are green, and most importantly they have land and water. They remember life in the refugee villages with disgust. "*Posti*[45] *kharab* (rotten)" spat out one woman. But women are proud to have participated in the *jihad*. One woman said, "I did *jihad*. My husband had a kalashnikov[46] and I cooked for all the men."

"My childhood was a dream and I would like to have the same time, like a queen without any problem or responsibility. [I married] when I was 16, gave birth one year later, then became a refugee. Twelve years we were in Legi Karez Dalbandin. My husband was Mujahid," Badamgul (35, HAZ 57).

During 1999, an increasing number of Hazara people left the Hazarajat in Afghanistan. Many of the refugees from this area pay smugglers to bring them across the border into Pakistan. One family had spent three months working as labour outside their village to afford to pay the smuggler his transportation fees. These new arrivals have crossed the border into the Baluchistan province of Pakistan and Iran. Quetta, the provincial capital, has a large Hazara population. They inhabit two areas of the city: Mariabad and Hazara Town. This population has built up over the last century due to the chronic food deficiency in the Hazarajat and persecution by neighbouring Pushtoon tribes. The majority of the agricultural land in the mountainous Hazarajat is rainfed, *lalmi*. Most farmers also have some irrigated land, *abi*. Due to low rainfall and water shortages, this *lalmi* land is not always able to support crops. Even in a good year of rain, small plots of land are not sufficient to feed the population of the area.

There are many landless people in the area who rely on livestock and labour on the lands of larger farmers, not just in their villages, but in the plains in Helmand, for instance. With the restrictions on movement by the Taliban, the Hazara men have been less able to travel for labour. This has made survival impossible for many families who have been forced to leave their villages as a result. Commodities are brought to the area on donkeys or horses. Families are unable to purchase those food goods that are in the bazaars because they are too expensive.

A few women said that they had come to Pakistan with their daughters due to rumours of Pushtoons taking young women. None of the new arrivals interviewed, men or women said that they knew a family to which this had happened. One of the women came across with her daughters, leaving all the male members of the family in Hazarajat. The men had found work on someone's farm and would not be paid until their labour was completed. People with significant amounts of land and livestock have often left some family members to tend to it.

---

[45] A refugee village in Dalbandin district of Baluchistan, Pakistan.
[46] AK 47 machine gun.

— 10 —

Conclusions

In addressing Afghan women's issues in the present environment, generalisations cannot be made. What can be said is that women's position under the present regime is not uniform. There are significant differences in urban and rural areas. The Taliban are stricter in areas that were more liberal during previous regimes.

The Taliban have taken a very extreme interpretation of religious and traditional Pushtoon practices, and in doing so they have changed the lives of many educated and working women completely. However, many rural women's lives have changed little. They were well acquainted with restricted mobility and the veil, either in the form of the *burqa* or *chadar*, prior to the Taliban.

It is important to distinguish between the rule of men and the rule of male (or Taliban) values. Though patriarchy, or the rule of the Taliban, may be considered gender oppression, it is also about power relations that are not always gender specific. Not all men in Afghan society dominate, and not all women are subordinate. Within their own spheres of power within the home, kin group, tribe, or village, some women dominate some men. For example, women will dominate men who are servants in their household, some women dominate their sons, sons-in-law and grandsons. What is going on in Afghanistan is not just an attack against women. Men are also being oppressed. Not all Afghan men are Taliban. It cannot be assumed, therefore, that all men in Afghanistan oppress all women.

In all research areas, women are permitted to move between compounds to visit relatives and female friends. Women get together for many activities: celebrations, condolences, and work. Older women are permitted more freedom outside the home than young women. But within their home villages, even young women are able to move around alone or with their children as *mahram*.

In areas where health care is available, women have access to these services. In more remote areas, the distances needed to travel for curative services, or in an emergency, are still great. Men are reluctant to make this journey until it is utterly necessary due to the expense and lost labour.

In rural Helmand, education was not appreciated prior to the war. There was also a lack of schools in rural Afghanistan. Now, access to female education is difficult and not seen by the majority of families as a top priority until basic needs are catered to first.

Refugee life has changed some of the priorities of Pushtoon women and their families. The value of education is high among refugees. Repatriated families and educated women complain that their children have been robbed of the opportunity for education. Even in areas such as Nawsad, where education was never prioritised, women and children have grown interested in education.

The desire to repatriate remains high among refugee families. Improved security in the south has enabled repatriation. However, uncertain means of livelihood, the devastation of family properties, the lack of education, and the Taliban's need for more male fighting power are concerns for families. The situation in the north is still confusing and violent.

It is clear from the narratives of these women that, though the majority are illiterate, they are not ignorant. Women have always had to negotiate their position within many systems and layers of power within their families, their culture and politics. Family influence continues to be important in determining issues concerning mobility, education and access to health care. For many rural and conservative urban women, the Taliban have been little more than one more layer of influence, and their lives have not been dramatically changed. For some, the inconvenience of the veil and additional restrictions are tolerated because the Taliban have provided security.

Within these layers of influence and power, women are able to operate, resist and comment on their lives in a number of very subtle ways.[47] These are ways in which women exercise their agency.[48] However, moving beyond the social value system is difficult for women in a community where family and male honour is tied to women's behaviour. There is concern about what others will say. Khadija (42, HAZ I) sums it up nicely:

"We want to hear more about everything but . . . we do according to society. We have a proverb: 'Eat what you want. Dress the way your community wants.' If we do something that is restricted in our community, the community will not like us."

The fact that Afghan women are not militant and now face many restrictions on their visibility and mobility does not mean they are passively doing nothing or would not like to do more to change their lives and those of future generations. The "veil" should not be considered an impermeable wall behind which there is no possibility for action. Instead, value and attention should be given to the voices of these women. For many rural women, it is only now that an awareness of the greater world (even within Afghanistan) and of their rights has begun to emerge. As the women themselves said, "We used to be like blind chickens. This is no more." It will be interesting to see what social animals with open eyes can achieve.

---

[47] An example of this is women weaving designs of weapons and slogans into carpets during the war.
[48] See Kumar 1994, Mernissi 1995, or Doubleday 1988.

Bibliography

Afkami, Mahnaz (ed.) (1995) *Faith & Freedom: Women's Human Rights in the Muslim World.* London: I.B Tauris.

Ahmed, Akbar S. (1976) "Millenium and Charisma Among Pathans," In *A Critical Essay in Social Anthropology.* London: Routledge & Kegan Paul.

Ahmed, Leila (1992) "Women and Gender in Islam," In *Historical Roots of a Modern Debate.* New Haven: Yale University Press.

Ali Majrooh, Parwin (1989) "Afghan Women Between Marxism and Islamic Fundamentalism," In *Central Asian Survey* Vol.8, no.3. London: Society for Central Asian Studies.

Arendt, Hannah (1985) *Imperialism: Part Two of the Origins of Totalitarianism.* London: Harcourt Brace & Company.

Bhabha, Homi. (1994) "Remembering Fanon: Self, Psyche and the Colonial Condition," In Patrick Williams & Laura Chrisman (eds.) *Colonial Discourse and Post-Colonial Theory.* London: Harvester and Wheatsheaf.

Boesen, Inger W. (1983) "Conflicts of Solidarity in Pakhtun Women's Lives," In Bo Utas (ed.) *Women in Islamic Societies: Social Attitudes and Historical Perspectives.* London: Curzon Press, Humanities Press.

Boesen, Inger W. (1988) "What Happens to Honour in Exile? Continuity and Change Among Afghan Refugees," In Bo Huldt, Erland Jansson (eds.) *The Tragedy of Afghanistan: The Social, Cultural and Political Impact of the Soviet Invasion.* London: Croom Helm.

Butler, Judith (1990) *Gender Trouble: Feminism and the Subversion of Identity.* London: Routledge.

Donnan, Hastings (1988) *Marriage Among Muslims: Preference and Choice in Northern Pakistan.* Leiden: E.J. Brill.

Doubleday, Veronica (1988) *Three Women of Herat*. London: Jonathan Cape.

Dupree, Nancy H. (1984) "Revolutionary Rhetoric and Afghan Women," In M.Nazif Shahrani and Robert L. Canfield (eds.) *Revolutions and Rebellions in Afghanistan: Anthropological Perspectives*. Institute of International Studies, Berkeley: University of California.

—— (1989) *Seclusion or Service: Will Women Have a Role in the Future of Afghanistan?* New York: Occasional Paper No.29. The Afghanistan Forum.

—— (1990) *Women as Symbols: Trends and Reactions*. Stockholm: The Swedish Committee for Afghanistan.

—— (1998) "Afghan Women Under the Taliban," In William Maley (ed.) *Fundamentalism Reborn? Afghanistan and the Taliban*. London: Hurst & Company.

Dupree, Nancy H., Anders Fänge, Anthony Hyman, Michael Keating, Olivier Roy (1999) *Afghanistan, Aid and the Taliban: Challenges on the Eve of the 21st Century*. Stockholm: The Swedish Committee for Afghanistan.

Grima, Benedicte (1993) "The Performance of Emotion Among Paxtun Women," In *The Misfortunes Which Have Befallen Me*. Karachi: Oxford University Press.

hooks, bell (1981) *Ain't I a Woman?* Boston: South End Press.

—— (1994) "Postmodern Blackness," In Williams, Patrick; Laura Chrisman (eds.) *Colonial Discourse and Post-Colonial Theory*. London: Harvester and Wheatsheaf.

Jayawardena, Kumari (1995) *The White Woman's Other Burden: Western Women and South Asia During British Rule*. London: Routledge.

Kumar, Nita (1994) "Introduction," In Nita Kumar (ed.) *Women as Subjects: South Asian Histories*. Charlottesville: University Press of Virginia.

Le Duc, Carol; Homa Sabri (1996) *Room to Maneuvre: Study on Women's Programming in Afghanistan.* Islamabad: UNDP.

Marsden, Peter (1999) *The Taliban. War, Religion and the New Order in Afghanistan.* Karachi: Oxford University Press.

Mernissi, Fatima (1987) *Beyond the Veil. Male–Female Dynamics in Modern Muslim Society.* Indianapolis: Indiana University Press.

Mernissi, Fatima (1995) *The Harem Within: Tales of a Moroccan Girlhood.* London: Bantam.

Mohanty, Chandra Talpade (1994) "Under Western Eyes: Feminist Scholarship and Colonial Discourses," In Williams, Patrick; Laura Chrisman (eds.) *Colonial Discourse and Post-Colonial Theory.* London: Harvester and Wheatsheaf.

Nair, Janaki (1992) "Uncovering the Zenana. Visions of Indian Womanhood in Englishwomen's Writings, 1813-1940." In Cheryl Johnson-Odim & Margaret Strobel (eds.) *Expanding the Boundaries of Women's Histor: Essays on Women in the Third World.* Bloomington & Indianapolis: Indiana University Press.

The Holy Quran

Said, Edward W. (1991) *Orientalism. Western Conceptions of the Orient.* London: Penguin.

Scott, Richard B. (1980) *Tribal and Ethnic Groups in the Helmand Valley.* Occasional Paper 21. New York: Afghanistan Council. The Asia Society.

Sedgwick, Eve Kosofsky (1990) *Epistemology of the Closet.* Berkeley: University of California Press.

Tapper, Nancy (1991) *Bartered Brides: Politics Gender and Marriage in an Afghan Ttribal Society.* Cambridge: Cambridge University Press.

Glossary

Abi   Irrigated land.

Badal   Exchange, reciprocity, revenge.

Baluch   Ethnic group in Baluchistan Province of Pakistan and border areas in Afghanistan and Iran.

Bazurk   Holy or religious person.

Burqa   A shuttlecock-shaped garment worn over the head with a net to see out of. Worn over clothes.

Chadar   A large shawl made from a variety of materials (cotton, polyester, wool) that is worn over clothing. Worn over the head, occasionally covering the face, or over the shoulders covering the upper body. Also known as *dupatta* or *polene.*

Chadari   Also known as *burqa,* see above.

Charas   Cannabis.

Dai   Traditional birth attendant.

Dasterkhan   Tablecloth. Cloth or plastic that food is laid out on for the meal on the floor.

Drishi   Condom. Literal translation: a man's suit.

Dum   Traditional curative method of saying words of the Quran and blowing at a person.

Dupatta   Also known as *chadar,* see above.

Eid   Muslim religious celebration.

Famil   Family, those who share the same resources and eat together.

Godar   Place for collecting water and washing clothes.

Hadith	Sayings of the Prophet Muhammed and his companions, one of the four sources of Islamic law.
Haj	Pilgrimage to Mecca.
Haram	Unlawful or forbidden, particularly by religious law.
Hashish	Cannabis.
Hazara	Ethnic group descended from Gengis Khan. The majority still inhabit the Hazarajat area in central Afghanistan, though Hazaras have spread into Pakistan and Iran.
Hijab	Long coat and head scarf that covers the whole body.
Hookah	Water pipe for smoking.
Ismaili	The Nizari Ismaili sect of Shi'ite Muslim community whose hereditary spiritual leader is the Aga Khan.
Izzat	Honour, respect.
Jihad	Holy war.
Kalashnikov	AK 47 machine gun.
Khan	Landlord, leader, elder.
Khanadan	All the people living in the same compound.
Khatme Quran	Silent individual or group reading of the Quran.
Koronai	Family, those who share the same resources and eat together.
Lalmi	Rainfed land.
Leef	Wash cloth.
Madrassa	School, religious school.

Mahram   Male family member who acts as company and protection for a woman when she moves outside her home.

Mardana   Male space in the home, or the men's side at a social gathering.

Mehr   Divorce compensation in Muslim marriage.

Mullah   Religious leader.

Mujahedin   Islamic freedom fighter.

Narina   Pushto term for male space in the home or the men's side at a social gathering.

Nikah   Marriage contract.

Nish   Lancing of poppy pods for opium.

Nuswar   Chewing tobacco.

Pir   Holy or religious person, saint.

Polene   Also known as *burqa*, see above.

Pshah Khalas   Contact between bride and groom before marriage ceremony.

Purdah   Veil, curtain, refuge, or hiding. The practice of women's seclusion and the segregation of the sexes.

Pushto   Language of the Pushtoon ethnic group.

Pushtoon   Largest ethnic group in Afghanistan, which inhabits areas along and on both sides of Pakistan–Afghanistan border.

Pushtoonwali   The complex Pushtoon cultural system of morality, modesty and law of honour. Also Pukhtunwali or Pukhtu.

Rahmat
Farishta   Angel of Blessing.

Sairatcha Male guestroom.

Shalwar Kamiz Shalwar are wide, gathered trousers, and *kamiz* is the tunic worn over them.

Shari'ah Islamic law.

Shezina Pushto term for female space in the home, or women's side at a social gathering.

Shia Muslims who believe that Hazrat-e-Ali is the first Khalifa after the Prophet Muhammed.

Sunni Muslims who believe that Hazrat-e-Ali is the fourth Khalifa after the Prophet Muhammed.

Talawat-e-Quran Group recitations of Quran out loud.

Tandoor Bread baking oven.

Taweez Amulet.

Wulluswal District Commissioner.

Wulwar Brideprice.

Zenana Female space in the home or women's side at a social gathering.

APPENDIX I

Interview Formats

Village Survey

Refugee village	Afghanistan
1. Why do you not go back to Afghanistan?	1. What do women think of the situation in Afghanistan?
2. What do women think of the situation in Afghanistan?	2. Access to health facilities? a. Now b. Before Taliban c. Before the War
3. Access to health facilities? a. Now b. Before Taliban c. Before the War	3. Access to education facilities? a. Now b. Before Taliban c. Before the War
4. Access to education facilities: a. Now b. Before Taliban c. Before the War	4. Influence of Taliban on daily life routine?
5. Influence of Taliban on daily life routine?	5. Comfortable with this influence? a. If not, why?
6. Comfortable with this influence? a. If not, why?	6. What is needed to be comfortable with life in Afghanistan?
7. What is needed to be comfortable with life in Afghanistan?	7. Can you work at home on income-generation activities? Outside the house? a. If yes, doing what types of work? b. If no, why not?
8. Can you work outside the house? a. If yes doing what type of work? b. If no, why not?	8. Can you grow vegetables in your compound (carrots, peppers, cabbage, spinach, olive, beans)?
9. Can you work at home on income-generation activities?	9. Can you raise small animals in your compound (chickens, rabbits, bees)?
10. Can you gow vegetables in your compound (carrots, peppers, cabbage, spinach, other)?	10. What is the view on training for women in: a. Health? b. Technical skills?
11. Can you raise small animals in your compound (chickens, rabbits, bees)?	

Refugee village	Afghanistan
12. What is the view on training for women in: a. Health? b. Technical skills?	11. Is it possible to give training to women in: a. Health? b. Technical skills?
13. Is it possible to give training to women in: a. Health? b. Technical skills?	12. How is it possible for training to be given in: a. Health, b. Technical skills
14. How is it possible for training to be given in: a. Health? b. Technical skills?	13. What would you like to learn to do? 14. What would you like to do?
15. What is the source of your information?	15. What is the source of your information?
16. How often do you get information from Afghanistan?	a. If men, who do they visit? Who visits them? b. Radio or TV? c. Weddings, parties, Mullah? d. Other?
Random surveys of 15 women in each of three refugee villages. Discussions with Health Committees.	

Gender Survey Questions

I. Details

1. Name
2. Age
3. Years married/unmarried/widowed
4. Number of members in the household/compound
5. Village
6. District

II. Life History Narratives

1. Where were you born and brought up?
2. Tell me about your childhood, how was life then?
3. How did things change as you grew older?
4. When were you married?
5. Did you give birth soon after the marriage? How were things then?
6. How many children do you have? ____Boys ____Girls
7. How have things changed as your children have grown older? Is their childhood different from yours? How?
8. How was life during the war?
9. When and why did you leave Afghanistan? *
10. Do you want to return? Why? Why Not? If you did you return, why? *
11. Tell me about your life now.
12. What sources of income does your family have now?

III. Women's Access to Education and Health Care

General Mobility and Access to Services

1. Are you allowed to go out of the house/compound/village for shopping/ bazaar, or to visit friends, or work in the fields/elsewhere? When and where do you go if you leave the house?

2. Do you travel outside the village/town to visit relatives/attend weddings/other celebrations? Where do you travel?

3. Do you go alone, with other women, with male relatives?

4. Was it easier to move around when you were younger or now?

5. Is that because of the situation in the village/country or because *purdah* has become more/less strict?

6. How did you do *purdah* in Afghanistan before the war/during the war? How do you do it now? Why?

Health Care

7. When you, your child or a relative is sick what do you do?

8. Where do you go for medical help? How is the health care?

9. Do you have any hospitals close to you?

10. Do you have to travel farther now than before for medical help?

11. Have you given birth? Where?

12. How has the hospital in Hazarjuft changed access to health care? Have you been there? How was it?

13. Was it different to give birth in Afghanistan than in the refugee village? Why? Difference before the war and after? Different during the war and now? *

Education

14. Have you gone to school? Where? What level?

15. Do your children go to school? Why? Why not?

16. Do/Did your brothers/husband go to school?

17. Do you go to *madrassa?* Who is teaching you there? What is taught? How often? How many women are there? Do young girls also go? Can you take your children there too?

18. How did you learn, or who taught you, to do housework and take care of children?

IV. Income-Generating Activities for Women

1. Do you do any income-generating activities (embroidery, sewing clothes, buying and selling cosmetics, creams, jewelry, cloth)?

2. Do you have time for income-generating activities? How much time do you have available for this or any new activities?

3. Is there any way your daily tasks could be speeded up to allow more time for income-generating activities?

4. Do husbands bring items for sale from Afghanistan/Pakistan? What items?

5. What items do you need? What could you sell?

6. What would you like to learn to do? What would be useful for you to know how to do?

7. What kinds of things could you sell or exchange with others in your community?

8. What would you need that is not available in your community?

9. Are there markets/bazaars close to you where you could buy and sell things?

10. What could you do inside or outside of the house?

11. Could you grow vegetables (carrots, cabbage, peppers, spinach, okra, beans, onions, tomatoes, melons) in the house/garden or on the roof?

12. Could you rear small animals (chickens, rabbits, bees, goats)?

13. If you grew vegetables or reared animals, could you sell your produce somewhere? Could your children or husbands sell it for you?

14. If training was available in the things you are interested in (health, technical skills, etc.) would/could you participate? If not, why?

15. If training in health and technical skills was given to you and other women in the community, where would be a good place for it to take place? Someone's home? Clinic? Outside in a compound?

V. Land

1. Do you have your own land? How much?

2. Do you have access to land?

3. How close/far away is your land?

4. What do you grow on your land?

5. How much vegetable/garden land does your family have in the compound?

6. How much vegetable/garden do you have outside the compound?

7. Do you personally have access to this land?

8. Do you ever help with work on this land? What do you do? What do the men do? What time of year?

9. How many fruit trees does your family own? What type of tree? How many of each type?

10. If you have fruit trees, what do you do with the fruit? Sell? Eat?

11. Is any of the fruit wasted? Why?

12. Do you grow poppy? How much land do you use for this?

13. Why do you grow poppy?

14. How do you sell poppy? In what form?

15. How much of your income comes from poppies?

16. Do members of your family do off-farm labour? Who does?

17. How much money do they earn with this?

18. How much time do they spend doing off-farm labour?

19. Where do they work as labourers?

20. How much of your income comes from other sources? What sources? How much from each?

21. How much wheat does your family need to eat each day/month?

22. How long does the food you grow on your land last? Is it enough for the whole year?

23. When you run out of food, where/how do you get more?

24. If we could increase your family income, would you still grow poppy? If yes, why? If no, why not?

Food for Work

1. Would you or your men agree to work for food?

2. If your husband was receiving food for work, how would women benefit?

3. What kind of work would you agree to do for food instead of money?

4. What type of male activity would women also benefit from? How?

V I. Women's Sources of Information

1. Who do you talk to? How often? Who don't you talk to? Why?

2. Do women get together often? For what occasions?

3. What kinds of things do you do together with other women? With your family?

4. Do you send children with messages to your neigbours or husbands?

5. Do you watch TV or listen to the radio?

6. Who do you visit? Why, when, and how often? Do you travel far?

7. Does your husband/son/brother/father or in-laws travel much? Into Afghanistan? Into Pakistan? Do they tell you about their travels? If so, what do they tell you?

8. Do you have relatives in other countries or elsewhere in Afghanistan/Pakistan? Are you in touch with them?

9. How do you keep in touch with relatives and friends in Afghanistan/Pakistan/elsewhere?

10. Are there many aid organisations/health clinics/community development people working in the community? Is your husband involved? If so, how? Are you involved? If so, how? Are you benefiting? If so, how?

VII. Repatriation*

1. What do you think of the situation in Afghanistan at the moment?

2. Do you want to move back to Afghanistan? Why or why not?

3. Have some of your family members already moved back?

4. Does your husband live in Afghanistan?

5. What would make your family decide to move back to Afghanistan?

6. What keeps you in Pakistan?

7. Do you know of people who have gone back to Afghanistan and then decided to come back to Pakistan again?

8. If you move back, will the whole family go back or just the men/women?

9. How would you go back?

10. Would you go back to your original village/city or live somewhere else in Afghanistan?

* Questions apply to refugee villages only.

APPENDIX II

Maps of Research Areas

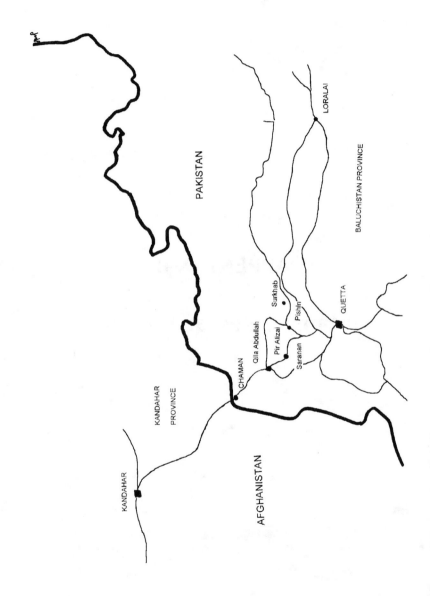

AFGHANISTAN

NAWSAD

GRISHK

Nad-i-Ali
LASHKARGAH

KANDAHAR

Arghandab River

Helmand River

KANDAHAR

PROVINCE

Hazarjuft
Mianpusta
Safar   Lakhi

Benader
Bagat

HELMAND

PROVINCE

QUETTA

CHAGAI DISTRICT

Chagai

NOSHKI

DALBANDIN

BALUCHISTAN PROVINCE

PAKISTAN

APPENDIX III

Details of Interviewees

Refugee Village Survey 1998

Code	Name	Village	District	Age
SAR 1	Gulbashra	Saranan	Killa Abdullah	
SAR 1	Wasia	Saranan	Killa Abdullah	
SAR 2	Kaldara	Saranan	Killa Abdullah	38
SAR 2	Tajdar	Saranan	Killa Abdullah	
SAR 3	Bibi Roqia	Saranan	Killa Abdullah	50
SAR 4	Halima (group)	Saranan	Killa Abdullah	46
SAR 4	Nazek	Saranan	Killa Abdullah	
SAR 4	Sharifa	Saranan	Killa Abdullah	
SAR 4	Shereen	Saranan	Killa Abdullah	
SAR 5	Bibi Ayesha	Saranan	Killa Abdullah	35
SAR 6	Bibi Hawa	Saranan	Killa Abdullah	49
SAR 7	Delbar (group)	Saranan	Killa Abdullah	43
SAR 8	Qadermanda	Saranan	Killa Abdullah	45
SAR 9	Zamarod	Saranan	Killa Abdullah	45
SAR 10	Nadira	Saranan	Killa Abdullah	52
SAR 11	Zarbibi	Saranan	Killa Abdullah	38
SAR 12	Gulpaida	Saranan	Killa Abdullah	
SAR 13	Negora (group)	Saranan	Killa Abdullah	32
SUR 1	Totia	Surkhab	Pishin	30
SUR 2	Bibi Ayesha	Surkhab	Pishin	28
SUR 3	Salma Bibi	Surkhab	Pishin	58
SUR 4	Belqisa	Surkhab	Pishin	30
SUR 5	Monawar	Surkhab	Pishin	48
SUR 6	Bibi Amina	Surkhab	Pishin	45
SUR 7	Sabira	Surkhab	Pishin	42
SUR 8	Sursandi	Surkhab	Pishin	35
SUR 9	Gul Babo	Surkhab	Pishin	
SUR 10	Belqis	Surkhab	Pishin	36
SUR 11	Hukoom Bibi	Surkhab	Pishin	
SUR 12	Safia	Surkhab	Pishin	38
SUR 13	Bibi Khatima	Surkhab	Pishin	
SUR 14	Bibi Rahima	Surkhab	Pishin	
SUR 15	Akhtar Bibi	Surkhab	Pishin	50

Interviewee Survey 1998

Code	Name	Village	District	Age	Marriage Age
HAZ 1	Khadija	Hazarjuft	Garamser	42	12
HAZ 2	Mahgula	Hazarjuft	Garamser	45	20
HAZ 3	Gulaba	Hazarjuft	Garamser	48	13 (widow)
HAZ 4	Bibigula	Hazarjuft	Garamser	55	15
HAZ 5	Zulaikha	Hazarjuft	Garamser	45	23
HAZ 6	Sharifa	Hazarjuft	Garamser	30	20
HAZ 7	Rangina	Hazarjuft	Garamser	95	15 (widow)
HAZ 8	Roshana	Hazarjuft	Garamser	35	15 (separated)
HAZ 9	Roqia	Hazarjuft	Garamser	38	23
HAZ 10	Hazrata	Hazarjuft	Garamser	55	20
HAZ 11	Rahmato	Hazarjuft	Garamser	35	15
HAZ 12	Lawangina	Hazarjuft	Garamser	15	Unmarried
HAZ 13	Amina	Hazarjuft	Garamser	25	22
HAZ 14	Adela	Hazarjuft	Garamser	20	10
HAZ 15	Najiba	Hazarjuft	Garamser	17	Unmarried
HAZ 16	Basira	Hazarjuft	Garamser	19	Unmarried
LAS 1	Bibigul	Lashkargah	Bust	70	20
LAS 2	Seema	Lashkargah	Bust	26	13
LAS 3	Bibi Gouhar	Lashkargah	Bust	45	12 (widow)
LAS 4	Shafiqa	Lashkargah	Bust	35	18
LAS 5	Sherinjan	Lashkargah	Bust	60	20
LAS 6	Khadija	Lashkargah	Bust	35	19 (widow)
LAS 7	Pekay	Lashkargah	Bust	25	18
LAS 8	Eqlima	Lashkargah	Bust	38	22
NAD 1	Shoogufa	Nad-i-Ali	Nad-i-Ali	38	18
NAD 2	Shah Bibi	Nad-i-Ali	Nad-i-Ali	70	14
NAD 3	Nazifa	Nad-i-Ali	Nad-i-Ali	38	Unmarried
GRI 1	Shahgul	Grishk	Nar-e-Saraj	52	19
GRI 2	Shahla	Grishk	Nar-e-Saraj	38	28
GRI 3	Hoor	Grishk	Nar-e-Saraj	65	15
GRI 4	Sakina	Grishk	Nar-e-Saraj	60	14

Code	Name	Village	District	Age	Marriage Age
GRI 5	Spozmai	Grishk	Nar-e-Saraj	40	24
GRI 6	Taj Bibi	Grishk	Nar-e-Saraj	56	16
GRI 7	Shahgul	Grishk	Nar-e-Saraj	40	29
GRI 8	Mohra	Grishk	Nar-e-Saraj	40	19
GRI 9	Bibigul	Grishk	Nar-e-Saraj	60	20 (widow)
GRI 10	Razia	Grishk	Nar-e-Saraj	40	16 (widow)
GRI 11	Torpekay	Grishk	Nar-e-Saraj	32	26
GRI 12	Marzia	Grishk	Nar-e-Saraj	50	15
GRI 13	Tahira	Grishk	Nar-e-Saraj	65	20 (widow)
GRI 14	Haji Khala	Grishk	Nar-e-Saraj	32	16
GRI 15	Noorjana	Grishk	Nar-e-Saraj	30	25
GRI 16	Shafiqa	Grishk	Nar-e-Saraj	18	15
PAZ 1	Sardara	Pir Alizai	Killa Abdullah	55	20
PAZ 2	Zelheja	Pir Alizai	Killa Abdullah	40	15
PAZ 3	Bibi Gul	Pir Alizai	Killa Abdullah	44	14

Interviewee Survey 1999

Code	Name	Village	District	Age	Marriage Age	Household Size
DB 1	Sabira	Deh Baloch	Nawsad	43	15 (widow)	
DB 2	Sherin	Deh Baloch	Nawsad	48	16	7
DB 3	Pakiza	Deh Baloch	Nawsad	45	13 (widow)	4
DB 4	Nikmargha	Deh Baloch	Nawsad	68	12 (widow)	15
DB 5	Gulzada	Deh Baloch	Nawsad	41	13	12
DB 6	Spozmai	Deh Baloch	Nawsad	30	13	12
DB 7	Bibi Gul	Deh Baloch	Nawsad	32	18	8
DB 8	Hussungula	Deh Baloch	Nawsad	44	24 (widow)	4
DB 9	Kubra	Deh Baloch	Nawsad	17	25	10
DB 10	Khayato	Deh Baloch	Nawsad	44	12	9
DM 1	Gulghotai	Deh Mian	Nawsad	20	22	13
DM 2	Ram Bibi	Deh Mian	Nawsad	59	16	9
DM 3	Sherina	Deh Mian	Nawsad	45	11 (widow)	7
DM 4	Qandi	Deh Mian	Nawsad	45	15	10
DM 5	Bibi Noor	Deh Mian	Nawsad	50	22	16
DM 6	Shabnam	Deh Mian	Nawsad	42	16	13
DM 7	Shafiqa	Deh Mian	Nawsad	20	10	3
DM 8	Babo	Deh Mian	Nawsad	58	14	9
DM 9	Shabnam	Deh Mian	Nawsad	44	18 (widow)	8
DM 10	Bibigula	Deh Mian	Nawsad	28	12	4
G 1	Bibi Aisha	Gena	Nawsad	40	13	7
G 2	Nikbakhta	Gena	Nawsad	50	15	11
G 3	Sharaba	Gena	Nawsad	42	22	13
G 4	Bora	Gena	Nawsad	30	20	11
G 5	Balanesta	Gena	Nawsad	42	20	13
G 6	Wasila	Gena	Nawsad	36	7 (widow)	3
G 7	Shamsa	Gena	Nawsad	40	Unmarried	8
G 8	Anargula	Gena	Nawsad	25	14	5
G 9	Gulan	Gena	Nawsad	50	18	18
G 10	Shakar	Gena	Nawsad	60	15	9
J 1	Khora	Jungolak	Nawsad	38	17	-
J 2	Mahgul	Jungolak	Nawsad	30	Unmarried	14

Code	Name	Village	District	Age	Marriage Age	Household Size
J 3	Jawahera	Jungolak	Nawsad	60	13 (widow)	5
J 4	Bibi Hoora	Jungolak	Nawsad	60	8 (widow)	5
J 5	Nasrin	Jungolak	Nawsad	30	15	11
J 6	Zamina	Jungolak	Nawsad	24	20	3
J 7	Babo	Jungolak	Nawsad	65	12	8
J 8	Gulmakai	Jungolak	Nawsad	38	20	13
J 9	Bibi Ayesha	Jungolak	Nawsad	50	9	-
J 10	Wasila	Jungolak	Nawsad	40	20	10
TA 1	Badro	Tangi Aulia	Nawsad	60	13 (widow)	6
TA 2	Amina	Tangi Aulia	Nawsad	38	10	11
TA 3	Shahwariza	Tangi Aulia	Nawsad	37	14	18
TA 4	Guldastan	Tangi Aulia	Nawsad	58	13	10
TA 5	Bibi Gula	Tangi Aulia	Nawsad	38	18 (widow)	6
TA 6	Wasila	Tangi Aulia	Nawsad	25	10	7
TA 7	Bibi Nazanin	Tangi Aulia	Nawsad	30	16 (widow)	8
TA 8	Zar Malik	Tangi Aulia	Nawsad	60	8	5
TA 9	Feroza	Tangi Aulia	Nawsad	42	12	17
TA 10	Khawiza	Tangi Aulia	Nawsad	38	15	5
HAS 1	Wolles Bibi	Shamalan	Garamser	25	14	7
HAS 2	Lawanga	Shamalan	Garamser	18	12	6
HAS 3	-	Shamalan	Garamser	40	12	15
HAS 4	Walat Bibi	Shamalan	Garamser	19	18	5
HAS 5	Khor Bibi	Shamalan	Garamser	18	10	5
HAS 6	Koko	Shamalan	Garamser	62	15	13
HAS 7	Bibi Amina	Shamalan	Garamser	22	12	5
HAS 8	Babo	Shamalan	Garamser	28	20	8
HAS 9	Nafasa	Shamalan	Garamser	28	10	6
HAZ 17	Painda	Hazarjuft	Garamser	40	12 (widow)	7
HAZ 18	Bibi Fatema	Hazarjuft	Garamser	40	13	9
HAZ 19	Kashmira	Hazarjuft	Garamser	60	15 (widow)	30
HAZ 20	Kashmira	Hazarjuft	Garamser	52	13	12
HAZ 21	Saltanat	Hazarjuft	Garamser	50	15 (widow)	5
HAZ 22	Azmat	Hazarjuft	Garamser	30	14	23
HAZ 23	Kemia Gula	Hazarjuft	Garamser	24	Unmarried	14
HAZ 24	Malika	Hazarjuft	Garamser	45	15	15
HAZ 25	Pargula	Hazarjuft	Garamser	18	28	20

Code	Name	Village	District	Age	Marriage Age	Household Size
HAZ 26	Khor Bibi	Hazarjuft	Garamser	20	23	8
HAZ 27	Saliqa	Hazarjuft	Garamser	19	18	9
HAZ 28	Khaldara	Hazarjuft	Garamser	62	10 (widow)	12
HAZ 29	Kawtar Bibi	Hazarjuft	Garamser	52	14	5
HAZ 30	Bibi Gula	Hazarjuft	Garamser	55	13	11
HAZ 31	Gulgulab	Hazarjuft	Garamser	40	15 (widow)	3
HAZ 32	Qandigul	Hazarjuft	Garamser	36	13 (widow)	9
HAZ 33	Bibi Tahira	Hazarjuft	Garamser	55	16	12
HAZ 34	Bibigula	Hazarjuft	Garamser	55	16	33
HAZ 35	Nadia	Hazarjuft	Garamser	40	13	13
HAZ 36	Khaldara	Hazarjuft	Garamser	49	10	20
HAZ 37	Dawlat	Hazarjuft	Garamser	52	15	13
HAZ 38	Zargara	Hazarjuft	Garamser	70	16 (widow)	6
HAZ 39	Rabia	Hazarjuft	Garamser	38	16	11
HAZ 40	Bibi Hawa	Hazarjuft	Garamser	51	17	10
HAZ 41	Lawangina	Hazarjuft	Garamser	18	17	8
HAZ 42	Gulsooma	Hazarjuft	Garamser	30	15	2
HAZ 43	Hazrata	Hazarjuft	Garamser	36	14	8
HAZ 44	Mahjan	Hazarjuft	Garamser	40	27	10
HAZ 45	Bibi Hazrat	Hazarjuft	Garamser	50	15	15
HAZ 46	Belqisa	Hazarjuft	Garamser	65	13	8
HAZ 47	Badam Gul	Hazarjuft	Garamser	25	15	5
HAZ 48	Hekmata	Hazarjuft	Garamser	40	13	8
HAZ 49	Zargara	Hazarjuft	Garamser	40	7	5
HAZ 50	Roshana	Hazarjuft	Garamser	35	13	15
HAZ 51	Zaiba	Hazarjuft	Garamser	70	15	10
HAZ 52	Roqia	Hazarjuft	Garamser	43	15	10
HAZ 53	Jawahir	Hazarjuft	Garamser	45	10	14
HAZ 54	Shah Bibi	Hazarjuft	Garamser	45	12	6
HAZ 55	Tamama	Hazarjuft	Garamser	40	18	25
HAZ 56	Gulsima	Hazarjuft	Garamser	25	13	9
HAZ 57	Badamgul	Hazarjuft	Garamser	35	14	16
HAZ 58	Shahperai	Hazarjuft	Garamser	50	13	15
KH 1	Hayat Bibi	Kharai	Garamser	38	7	7
WO 1	Bibi Zar	Woleswaly	Garamser	26	12	8
DZ 1	Tajdar	Deh Zekria	Garamser	37	18	14

Code	Name	Village	District	Age	Marriage Age	Household Size
DZ 2	Badama	Deh Zekria	Garamser	35	20	13
DZ 3	Khora	Deh Zekria	Garamser	53	10	10
DA 1	Hukum Bibi	Darweshan	Garamser	40	15	8
DA 2	Kheshmesh	Darweshan	Garamser	70	14	10
DA 3	Durkhanai	Darweshan	Garamser	48	16 (widow)	9
DA 4	Bibi Borjana	Darweshan	Garamser	30	7	10
LO 1	Bulbula	Loy	Garamser	41	9	9
LO 2	Bibi Zahra	Loy	Garamser	23	14	7
LO 3	Bibi Nahida	Loy	Garamser	20	12	4
LO 4	Feroza	Loy	Garamser	22	14	6
L 1	Sahiba	Laki	Garamser	60	14 (widow)	5
L 2	Badro	Laki	Garamser	41	15	10
L 3	Zargula	Laki	Garamser	21	10	5
L 4	Rasto	Laki	Garamser	37	20	13
L 5	Bakhtawar	Laki	Garamser	20	28	5
L 6	Guldana	Laki	Garamser	19	14	5
CH 1	Shirina	Chagai	Chagai	55	20	20
CH 2	Alam Bibi	Chagai	Chagai	20	14	13
CH 3	Bibi Hosha	Chagai	Chagai	35	10	12
LK 1	Zardana	Legi Karez	Chagai	35	15 (widow)	4
LK 2	Lal Bibi	Legi Karez	Chagai	35	10	9
P 1	Ram Bibi	Posti	Chagai	38	10	14
P 2	Zar Bibi	Posti	Chagai	38	10	15
P 3	Sanam	Posti	Chagai	30	14	8

APPENDIX IV

Agricultural Production and Livestock

Northern Helmand Province

Type of Production

Crops	Wheat
	Corn
	Cumin
	Poppy
	Alfalfa
Fruit	Apple
	Peach
	Apricot
	Mulberry
	Pomegranate
	Almond
	Grapes
	Figs
	Melon
Vegetables	Eggplant
	Okra
	Cauliflower
	Onions
	Spinach
	Tomatoes
	Mint
	Peppers
Livestock	Chickens
	Cows
	Goats
	Turkeys
	Donkeys
	Rabbits

Products: Wheat Flour, Corn Flour, Cumin, Opium, Animal Feed, Fresh and Dried Fruit, Nuts, Vegetables, Herbs, Eggs, Meat, Milk, Lassi, Yoghurt, Meat, and Transportation.

Southern Helmand Province

Type of Production

Crops
Wheat
Corn
Cotton
Poppy
Mong Beans
Alfalfa

Fruit
Apple
Mulberry
Pomegranate
Watermelons
Melon
Apricot
Almond
Grapes

Livestock
Chickens
Cows
Goats
Turkeys
Donkeys
Rabbits
Sheep
Ducks

Vegetables
Eggplant
Okra
Cauliflower
Onions
Spinach
Tomatoes
Mint
Chili Peppers
Cabbage
Cucumber
Potatoes
Pumpkin
Carrots
Garlic
Turnips
Radish

Products: Wheat Flour, Corn Flour, Cotton, Opium, Beans, Animal Feed, Fresh and Dried Fruit, Seeds, Nuts, Oil, Vegetables, Eggs, Meat, Milk, Yoghurt, Wool, and Transportation.

NOTES

NOTES

Helping Afghanistan's Women and Children

Since 1986, Mercy Corps has worked with the Afghan people, providing food, jobs, medicine and hope for millions of people who have suffered through years of drought, conflict and social unrest.

Mercy Corps' programs in Afghanistan are aimed at addressing the immediate and long-term needs of families and communities. These include:

- **Health** - Mercy Corps maintains a system of hospitals and rural basic health units (BHUs) which provide maternal and child health care to more that 145,000 women and children in Afghanistan and Afghan refugees in Pakistan.

- **Agriculture** - Mercy Corps works to improve seed qualities and supplies as well as irrigation systems.

- **Refugee Assistance and Repatriation** - Mercy Corps provides direct relief assistance to hundreds of thousands of internally displaced persons, as well as Afghan refugees living in Pakistan.

- **Disabled Persons** - Mercy Corps provides physiotherapy and prosthetic devices to Afghan refugees in Pakistan as well as the local population.

- **Infrastructure** - Mercy Corps works to rehabilitate neglected vital structures such as hospitals and bridges.

- **Food** - Mercy Corps distributes emergency food supplies to Afghans affected by armed confli

Mercy Corps exists to alleviate suffering, poverty and oppression by helping people build secure productive and just communities. Since 1979, Mercy Corps has provided over $576 million in assistance to 73 nations. Mercy Corps is a nonprofit organization with headquarters offices in: Portland, Oregon; Seattle, Washington; Washington, DC; and Edinburgh, Scotland. Over 95 perc of the agency's resources are allocated directly to programs that help those in need.

- -

Please use my enclosed contribution to help children and families in need in Afghanistan and other neighboring countries.

❏ $500   ❏ $100   ❏ $50   ❏ Other_____

❏ Please send me the *Mercy Report*, an electronic update about Mercy Corps' programs.

_____
name

_____
address

_____
city/state/zip

_____
email address

 **Mercy Corps**

mercycorps.org

Thank You! *Please make your check payable to* **Mercy Corps**,
*PO Box 2669, Portland, OR 97208-2669. It you have any questions,
call (800) 292-3355, ext. 250, or visit www.mercycorps.org.
Your lifesaving gift is tax-deductible to the full extent of the law.*

3100/B